99 Girdles on The Wall

a memoir

by
Elena Louise Richmond

Back cover artwork: © Hilaire Squelette, the cartoonist name of artist Madelaine Ramey.

Front cover painting: © Elena Louise Richmond, "Final Resting Place of James Knott, Gunnislake, Cornwall."

Cover photographs © Elena Louise Richmond.

Book and Cover Design by Vladimir Verano, Third Place Press

ISBN: 978-1-60944-041-1

 at Third Place Press, Lake Forest Park, on the Espresso Book Machine v.2.2.
thirdplacepress.blogspot.com
www.thirdplacepress.com

For Doug

who heard all these stories first

My aunt Frances and I were recounting the events of our day to my Uncle Don when Frances turned to me and said, in astonishment, "Why Lainie, you're lying!"

"I am not. I'm elaborating. To make a better story."

"You're just lying."

Some of the names, locations, and particulars have been elaborated to protect the innocent author.

God bless the child that's got her own

I WAS BORN TO BE MIDDLE-AGED. I was 53 the year my mother died. By the end of her life, I had a surge of possibilities for my own. After her death, I was able to consider the possibility that she had loved me.

For her estate sale, I nailed my mother's twenty-seven girdles to the wall of her bedroom. Girdles, instruments of torture that impede the breath and imprison joy, were emblematic of her repressive influence. Even when she lay dying, she had the energy to tell me to put my knees together.

In the first nine hours of cleaning out her bedroom, I waded through magazines, lengths of fabric, eight by ten glossies of the Reagan and Nixon families, rolls of toilet paper, shoes, religious books, laundry, and the kitchen overflow of raisin bran and cornflake boxes to get to the dresser where I found the girdles. Big industrial size girdles. One of them was pink. I found piles of individual garters. My mother had tried for a time to make girdles. She hated to spend money for any reason.

"I can make that for so much less." She said this about everything: coats, swim suits, underwear, restaurant desserts, oil paintings.

My singing student, Anna, was with me the day we hung things on the walls. We needed floor space to display sixty years, three floors and five bedrooms of my mother's glorious junk. Anna hung pictures and posters until the walls were covered. Then we got the bright idea of nailing all twenty-six girdles to the bedroom wall. I added signs: "99 girdles on the wall, take one down, pass it around."

I made a time-line from what I found amongst the girdles. I found a tiny-waisted black skirt with a note attached: "I was wearing this skirt when I met your dad. Waist: 21 inches." I found love letters between my parents that I never dreamed existed, all dated during the first year of their marriage before the babies arrived. I found my christening gown and the baby announcements from the Seattle Times for my brother, Alex, and myself.

I collected little Sunday school things: book marks, prayer cards, cards with the Beatitudes, the Lord's Prayer, the Twenty-Third Psalm; four pins that said "perfect attendance," with tiny military-looking bars added for the second, third and fourth years. Everyone in the family got a perfect attendance pin during the years that we were all in the Lord's Army and Right with God. There were pins that said "I brought One," or "I brought Two" for when we had picked up a lost sheep or two on our way to church.

There were hundreds of books in the house. When I was a child I played Librarian. I made library cards for the books I thought had interesting titles. My father gave me a date stamper and stamp pad so I could serve my imaginary library patrons. I found some of those library cards in my mother's bookshelf. My child's hand had written "Of Human Bondage" and "Lonely but Not Alone." I looked at them for a long time. These were titles that intrigued me when I was a child.

I tried to sort the religious books apart from the others but there were religious books everywhere. They infiltrated every bookcase, trying to evangelize the rest of the books in the house. I stacked three hundred of them on the front porch in the hopes they'd be stolen.

I picked up a book called *Please Love Me* by Keith Miller. It was a story of a woman who was raped and then something Christian happened to her. On the front cover was a picture of the heroine running down the street in the snow. I never read the book but my mother pushed it on me urgently when I was about to start high school.

"Elena. You *must* read this book."

Rape, prostitution, and illegitimate children stood between me and this book.

"I am not reading your *stupid* book!"

"Mary, leave her alone about the book," my father intervened.

"Why can't she do *one thing* for me?" my mother fumed.

As I blew the dust off the book and flipped its pages, checking for the cash my mother tended to leave in books she thought I needed to read, I mused on why my reading a book would be doing something for my mother. I asked her once if she thought she had been sexually abused. For once, she didn't give me one of her repressive looks.

"No, I don't think so. I would have remembered."

That's exactly what she wouldn't have done. That she seemed to have already considered the idea was significant.

I recalled some of her weird comments about sex, and the frenzy she could get into: "When you get pregnant, don't think you can come back into this house!"

Or the day she barged into my room apropos of nothing while I was reading a *Tiger Beat*, which I chucked under the bed, and said, "Elena. Don't ever talk about menstruation in front of a boy."

I found piles of old-fashioned bobby pins. They brought back some ugly memories: my mother's monthly "spa treatments" starting when I was eight or nine, continuing into my teens until I refused to cooperate: She positioned herself in bed and called for me to "come scratch my dandruff." This meant I was to climb into bed with her, find patches of hard ground in her scalp, and plow them with a comb. Then she had me stick a bobby pin in her ear and scoop out the wax and dried skin. Finally she would roll on her stomach so I could squeeze the blackheads on her back. I worked assiduously at these tasks. They seemed no more strange to me than the times she asked me to smell her body: her breath, her armpits, her crotch.

I found dozens of pairs of white gloves from the 50s, dozens of elaborate rhinestone star burst pins, and her occupational therapist pins, patches and certificates. I searched for a long time before I found a pink faux pearl and rhinestone necklace that I had given my mother for her forty third birthday. I was seven. She and I were shopping in Frederick and Nelsons where I had a secret meeting with the clerk at the jewelry counter. I picked out the necklace, the clerk wrapped it up with a conspiratorial smile, and my mother paid for it.

The necklace had come unstrung just as our relationship had, but my mother had preserved it in its box. She may not have remembered its significance, but nothing else among her stuff was in its original box.

I found stacks of recital programs from years of childhood piano lessons and more professional looking ones from my voice recitals and concerts as an adult. Some were annotated in my father's peculiar, spidery hand. He made the body of his letters small and cramped but looped and swirled the appendages. The ink was fading on his glowing assessment of me and my singing.

There was a program with me singing the Queen of the Night's revenge aria from The Magic Flute. I didn't expect to find that program in my mother's bedroom. I thought I had stopped inviting my parents to my performances by then.

In my 30s, I had a bright, flexible coloratura that soared once it got passed high G. I could race up another octave to A-flat, but the high F in the revenge aria was my public high note. It's unusual to get all the Fs in that piece. Even after years of training in those upper reaches, I only managed one good clear pierce of the stratosphere per performance.

Two of my piano students, elementary school-aged boys, ran up to me after a concert to ask, "How did you get it to beep like that?"

Thousands of hours of practice and tens of thousands of dollars for lessons to learn to ring a crystalline bell tone on any note with any vowel and they want to know how I got it to beep! I smiled and tossed the programs onto the recycle pile already loaded with Hour of Decision and *Good Housekeeping* magazines.

Good Housekeeping. I diagnosed myself as depressed at age 10 when I read a woman's story in one of my mother's *Good Housekeeping*. The woman described feelings that I felt: sadness, a dull dread, and the sense that something was wrong but there were no words to describe it and no one to listen. The article called it "depression." The woman in the story was undergoing psychoanalysis. I thought that maybe one day, I would go to an analyst. I was always deeply frightened that something terrible was going to happen to me if I didn't do the right things, but I couldn't know ahead of time what those right things were. What I didn't understand was that the terrible thing was happening right then. I was having my childhood. There was little escape or comfort.

I pulled a hat box off the shelf of the bedroom closet and five $20 bills rained down on me. Searching further, I found a Sucrets tin stuffed with $900. That was it for the money, though I opened every single book in the house and checked for bills. My brother, Alex, and I had earlier counted and divided about $500 in change, hidden in baby food jars in my mother's underwear drawers.

There was less exalted stuff in the house: 32 rolls of paper towels, 65 packages of toilet paper, 28 cans of Comet, 27 five-pound bags of flour, bug infested; 16 five-pound bags of sugar. There were two army issue file cabinets in the basement. One drawer was packed with boxes of damp, hardened Jello; one drawer had rows of powdered sugar boxes, another of brown sugar, all brick hard. Another drawer was the overflow drawer for bags of chocolate chips, the main supply being upstairs, filling several kitchen drawers. There was a drawer for bags of rice, lentils, and beans. There were damp boxes of cold cereal, and cases of canned soup, much of it dating back to before there were sell dates. The most suspicious stuff was in Mason and Kerr jars, no longer resembling anything edible. We made 15 dump runs in the course of the cleanup and disposed of 84 pounds of inedible food.

I found two reams of full size Arches 130 lb, cold pressed watercolor paper. That was more exciting than the $1000 because it was so unexpected. Late in her life, my mother had astonished us all by taking up watercolor painting and showing some ability. I especially admired the way she did evergreen trees. She did a credible pine tree with just a dab or two of the brush. Or a whole line of distant fir trees with a few moves. My father bought a mat cutter and framed all her best pieces.

After my father died, I learned to paint and I encouraged my mother to continue painting. I wanted her to teach me how to do those lines of trees that I admired. It would give us something to do together. But she said she had too much else to do.

"Like what?"

"Well, I don't want to leave this house full of stuff for you kids to clean out when I die," she said.

It was highly doubtful that "you kids" would be cleaning out the house. My brother had no interest in it. If it had been left up to him, he would have sold everything to a dealer without lifting a single box flap. I, on the other hand, had been itching to get my hands on the junk in that house since we moved into it forty-five years earlier. The knowledge of this unnerved my mother. Once I saw her feet sticking out of her bedroom closet as she burrowed to its depth. She emerged, waving a box of those cards that used to come with nylon hose, "Chuuuck! When I die, don't let Elena throw these out!"

I was a great declutterer. I was always trying to find more breathing room for myself, always sorting what did and did not have meaning for me. When my brother left home, leaving the entire second floor uninhabited, I moved into the spacious attic bedroom at the top of the house. I sorted and packed, then tried to get the boxes past my mother and into the three-on-a-tree Rambler, the car I drove, and thence to Goodwill.

My parents were talking in the kitchen one afternoon when I was ready to disgorge some possessions from the upstairs. Because I would never get the stuff past my mother, I tied ropes around the boxes and lowered them out the window to the back yard. Then I walked innocently through the kitchen and out to the car. My father met me in the driveway, his face full of amusement, having seen the boxes go past the kitchen window.

He knew exactly what I was doing because he did much the same thing on a different front. Under the basement stairs were fifteen boxes with lids, all of them marked *Harvard Classics,* a label guaranteed to deter my mother. The boxes were full of right-wing political and religious solicitations. My father added to them by the fistful, as he made trips downstairs. Every week, he emptied as much as would fit into the garbage before hauling the can to the street for collection.

After my father died, my mother asked me to help her pack his clothes. But shortly after we started turning out his closet, she said, "I think I'll go sit down in the other room for a while." Her face was pale and strained as she crept away. The most she would say was, "Well there's nothing I can do about it. We all die." So I cleaned out his bedroom and the den where he had listened to Wagner and messed around on his computer while my mother played endless games of solitaire in the front room.

The last time I saw my mother, she was still able to slump in a sitting position. She insisted on using a commode instead of a bed pan—it was a dignity thing, the nurses told me—and it took two aides about an hour to get her through a toilet call. I arrived toward the end of one such call. She looked at me disapprovingly. I walked out to let them clean her up and tuck her in a wheelchair.

She was glowing iridescent yellow, like a cartoon character, but I was used to her jaundice. What shocked me was how shrunken she had become. I sat next to the wheelchair and sang a few songs to her. She smiled at the religious ones but frowned when I sang some of her first grader songs like "Six little ducks that I once knew" or "Wake up little Pilgrims the sun is in the east." It was a frown of confusion, I thought, not disapproval. I don't think she remembered them though she taught them for 45 years.

I wheeled her out into the hall and we started a tour of the Hospice center. "Let's go to the end," she murmured, gesturing slightly down the hall. "See what's there." She pointed to an exit sign: "Exit," she said. To a clock: "It's time." I was fascinated by the stream of references coming out of her.

She announces to everyone that she's dying," the nurses told me. "She seems proud of it."

The day came when the hospice nurse called to say she gave my mother another 48 hours. She had seen her that morning. She was unresponsive but there had been a bit of a bowel movement.

"That's nice," I said, "She loved her bowel movements." The nurse started to laugh, which made me think I might become hysterical.

I requested a Hospice volunteer to sit with my mother round the clock until her death, a vigil I was not emotionally equipped to keep. So it happened that I called the next afternoon and asked the volunteer to hold the phone to my mother's ear so I could talk to her, even though she was "unresponsive."

Then I didn't know what to say.

So I said, "I love you, I love you, I love you, I love you, I love you, I love you."

I didn't know what I meant. I hung up.

Ten minutes later, Hospice called to say my mother had died just after the phone call. Tears had been seeping out from under her eyelids. It was the day before Thanksgiving. She was 89 years old.

I canceled my afternoon piano students but two of them—brothers—showed up anyway with their manny and a friend of theirs whom I didn't know. All four of them had made condolence cards. The manny must have told them to write: "I'm sorry for your loss" because all the cards said this. The boys had drawn flowers and signed their names. They were lovely. The one child I didn't know had evidently thought through his position carefully because on his card he added a helpful post-script: "You met me." This made me laugh until I gave way to tears at last.

I went for a walk. A block from my house, my mother found me. I felt weightless and I suddenly thought, "I don't feel guilty." Simultaneously, I heard my mother's abrasive, scolding voice say what she had said in response to every feeling I had ever had:

"There's no reason to feel that way."

I laughed outright. She was there and in spite of the harsh tone, I felt love wash through me.

The love-saturated feeling stayed with me for weeks after her death. When my mother's spirit was freed from her tortured mind, she gave me what she had never been able to give me in life and what I had never been able to receive: A mother who loved me. There began a subtle re-working of the mother image I carried around inside me. I started to feel internally the mother I had needed and wanted, not the mother I had had. My memories weren't different. It's not like I thought, "Oh, it wasn't so bad." I didn't. I knew and remembered how bad it had been. But the memories started to mean something different.

Tiny Tears

A WOMB IS A PRIZED PIECE OF REAL ESTATE: *enclosed space with privacy walls, breathes for you, nutrients included.* I believe I enjoyed being in the womb because ever since I began breathing and eating on my own, I have felt a pull backward—or forward, whatever it took—to anything that would be better than this life. I have always felt drawn to womb-y things like barns, woods, warm beds, and graves. As a child, I was enchanted by cemeteries. I spent 4o years wanting my own death; after I decided I preferred to live, I moved into a house that abutted a cemetery and had a gate put in.

In life outside the womb, my body got little attention. My mother liked to tell the story—as reported to her by the woman in the neighboring hospital bed—of repeatedly babbling, while coming out of ether, "Thank you God for giving me a little girl."

I asked her why she wanted a little girl.

"I wanted to make clothes for you," she said.

I don't remember how that worked out when I was very young, but when I was older, she fit my clothes to her body. When they didn't fit me, she said,

"Well, you're short waisted."

Between my mother and myself, there was just the one body, long after I had left her womb by Caesarian section. Her indigestion was mine: "We don't eat onions, do we?" And here's an after dinner classic: "I have a headache. Do you have a headache? What did we eat that gave us a headache?"

I'll take a stab at answering the question of why my mother wanted a little girl. She wanted someone to know her story, and since she had lost the ability to tell it outright, it was going to be told through her daughter's life. However I am not going to tell my mother's story. God knows I tried to live it out for her and that didn't work. I am going to tell my own story.

When I was born, my family lived in Bellevue, Washington, which in the 1950s was a cow town across Lake Washington from Seattle. We lived in an old red house with a fish pond and the occasional fish and frogs collected from Lake Washington. My parents bred German Shepherds for a couple of rounds until they ended up with a puppy they kept. They wanted to give the dog a German name and they came up with Una. I always thought that was sweet because I considered it the first and last imaginative thing my parents did.

My brother, Alex, preceded me by 18 months. He was named Alexander after my mother's father, Georg Alexander Kiosse and my mother's favorite brother, Alec. Everyone called my brother Alex except my mother. "I named him *Alexander*," she said until the day she died.

Alex did not welcome the competition for our parents' attention. According to family legend, he wanted me to go back where I came from. As already noted, I was ambivalent on that point myself. In any case, most of my early memories are of me, alone. I don't remember other people being there.

I can still feel the rough wood floor of the living room that gave way to the cool of the kitchen linoleum as I crawled through the house, rolling marbles and balls. I pinned my dolls by their hair to the clothesline. I sat in the raspberry patch and binged on the raspberries.

I had a knitted green blanket in which I had worn a hole big enough to make it a poncho. I wore the green blanket and carried my Tiny Tears doll everywhere. Tiny Tears was a brand of doll that came with a tiny baby bottle. When it was fed, the liquid would seep out its eyes. A doll whose raison d'etre was to cry. I never gave my doll another name. I always called her Tiny Tears.

I held Tiny Tears when, at age three, they stuck me on the platform at Highland Covenant Church to sing "Jesus Loves Me." I wasn't frightened up there, staring at those adult faces. I was already an old woman looking backwards to see ahead. I would be a singer but singing would not be about performing for others. Singing would be my reassurance that I was alive, that I was still breathing, and that life was resonating within me.

At age seven my big hits were "Let the sunshine in, face it with a grin," and "I'll Be a Sunbeam for Jesus." Those were my public songs but they could have been disguises for Halloween.

I had a private song that I sang just for me. The words went like this:

When He cometh, when He cometh to take up his jewels,

All His jewels, precious jewels, His loved and His own.

Like the stars of the morning, His bright crown adorning,

They shall shine in their beauty, bright gems for His crown.

I am appalled now at the narcissism of the God in this song, but as a little girl, I was mostly interested in those morning stars. They shone brightly, they had something to do with being loved and they were far away. I hoped to find them someday and this is why the song was private: my parents had a way of co-opting my desires into service to themselves. If there was something I wanted, I had to figure out how to get it on my own because they had their own preoccupations.

How Infirm a Foundation

DURING MY FIRST SEVEN YEARS, my father drank vodka, heavily and secretly. I don't remember seeing a single bottle although my mother was always dispatching me to try and catch him in the act. "Go out to the garage and see if he is"—stage whisper uttered in my face—"DRINKING." I never saw him take a drink but I learned to calculate the stages of drunkenness as hour by hour, he would reappear among us, trying to act normal: The smell, the slurring of words, the bloodshot eyes, the topics he decanted when he was drunk, and his addressing me as "friend." By the time I was his "friend," he was about finished for the day and it was my bedtime.

He was an ugly drunk. He raved and lurched around the house. He blocked the door and wouldn't let our friends through until they answered the question, "Do you believe in God?" He could be fierce when drunk and goaded. My mother goaded. She poked and nagged until he erupted. Then she sat back smugly and said, "Well, that's a fine way for a grown man to behave."

My father was born in Walla Walla, Washington, the grandson of immigrants from England and Sweden. His mother, Louise Knott, of the early Walla Walla Knotts, married Charles Richmond—those damn wheat farmers in Prescott—and together they had four boys. Louise died of the Spanish flu in 1918 when my father was eight years old. Charles died five years later from gall bladder disease. The boys were raised by Louise's sister, Ann. Aunt Ann. She was the closest thing I knew to a grandmother. A fussy old Victorian, she was, in other ways, a rebel. She went off to France to nurse during the First World War against her father's wishes and didn't marry until she was 45 years old.

Nowhere did my mother's feelings of inferiority whine more forcefully than in relation to Aunt Ann.

"Born with a silver spoon in your mouth. You and Aunt Ann."

My father countered with, "At least you *had* parents. I was an orphan."

Myths sprang up over how my father stopped drinking. My father always maintained that he was up one night reading Einstein's theory of relativity and something fell into place inside him. After that he didn't take another drink for 13 years (his estimation) or three years (my mother's). My mother's story was that he was up one night, prowling around with his chronic insomnia, and he had a vision of the Lord coming to him in a great light, telling him to stop drinking, and so he did. Just like that.

Thus, when I was seven, began the Richmond family's golden age. When we were all Right With God. When nightly, the family prayed together, on our knees in the living room, speaking in Middle English. My brother had a speech tweak where he said his *ch*'s with an excessive amount of mouth juice, which irritated me; and my mother made all kinds of superfluous mouth noises when she talked so I tried to kneel far away from them and I plugged my ears when she prayed or when I thought my brother might possibly be coming up on the word *church*.

My father's prayers always began with "Our Father, we thank thee for all thy many blessings."

My mother's prayers always ended with "Guide and direct us in all thy ways." She also went in for a lot of sighing. She wanted God to know what a huge burden she was carrying down here and but for her recalcitrant family, she could do better.

After my father started drinking again—either 3 or 13 years later— my mother, whenever she got into a pique, referred back to the days when we were Right With God. When I was older, and she went into a tirade about the how awful we were—*Stinking* being the descriptor— since we had Gotten Away From God, I could throw her rant in the ditch by commenting,

"I hated all those times we had to pray together. It was horrible."

Mid-roar, she could be silenced for a few seconds, followed by the dark statement: "What You Kids Need is a Good Depression."

I did grow up to have a good depression, one that lasted about 45 years, although I believe at the time, she was referring to the one in the 1930s.

My mother came of age during the 1930s depression in Eastern Montana, 60 miles south of Miles City, the child of Bulgarian immigrants who were as stern and unforgiving as the land they homesteaded. The family was of the Greek Orthodox faith. The priests came around with their icons and robes every so often and set up services in the one room country schoolhouse. But my mother, like me, like most of us, got the God of our religious indoctrination mixed-up with our parent's personalities. From what I can make out, my grandfather was a terrifying individual, and my grandmother was a terrified and unhappy woman.

As was my mother. Up until the month before she died, I had few images of her face except one contorted in rage. She was always furious about something; something as innocuous as my announcing in the car-ride to church that I was not wearing underwear. It could be rage at the general immorality of the world or the price of onions.

My brother and I could easily set her off. "K-I-I-D-S," she screamed, making the word as long as the fireplace poker that she would occasionally brandish at us. "God is going to punish you!"

She tried guilt: "Before I had children, I told myself I was never going to yell at them."

She didn't have to elaborate. I was a child. I knew it was all my fault.

Religion was my mother's life support; the Bible, her respirator. Every breath she took was first cycled through her King James Bible, which was *the* word of God. The other ones were not, and especially not the Living Bible, which used the word *intercourse* when explaining that the Virgin Mary had not had It. The King James word of God told you how to live your life and how to measure other members of the human race so as to take comfort in your spiritual superiority, although you could not admit this to your daughter.

I used to try to get my mother to specify one thing she had ever done wrong, ever, in her entire life.

"Nothing," she would say with a red face and an uncomfortable giggle; she was never comfortable with sarcasm, or humor, really.

Late in her life, when she was in her 80s, she amended that position to concede that her house could have been cleaner. And that was not sarcasm. That was all she could come up with. In 80 years.

Getting Saved

WE WERE BORN AGAIN CHRISTIANS. We had accepted Jesus as our personal savior. I personally, did so several times, because I was never clear whether it had stuck. The first time I remember was at age seven. My mother always insisted I had repented of my sins and received Jesus into my heart when I was four. She had been there, although I don't remember any of it. What seems credible is that I got stuck on the word *repent*. Or *sins*. In any case, she wasn't there to officiate at subsequent conversions so she didn't think they had happened.

At age seven, I was sitting in that dreadful phenomenon known as Sunday School, kicking my heels against a chair, full of anxiety that I might be going to hell. Alex had told me that there was a thing called the "age of consent" and it was Age Six. It meant that you had a Get Out of Hell Free card on all sin up to age six. After that, if you died with unconfessed sin or weren't saved at all, you would go straight to hell. So I prayed to Jesus to come into my heart if He wasn't there already. Starting now. This time for real. I didn't know if I had done it right. I didn't feel different.

At another dreadful phenomenon, a Billy Graham crusade, I felt "convicted by the Holy Spirit," which meant I felt guilty about being alive at all. It was a heightening of the thing I carried with me all the time: something terrible was going to happen. When you got this feeling, at a crusade or a garden variety altar call, you were supposed to go to the front and get down on your knees and someone would tell you how to be saved, how to be washed in the blood of the lamb and receive Jesus as your personal saviour. I did not want to go down front, and my mother wanted it even less than I did because she didn't want to get stuck in traffic on the way home.

"You were saved when you were four," she said. "Get your coat on."

Christian radio played all day long at our house whether we liked it or not, and we didn't. There was a program called *The Haven of Rest* with First Mate Bob and the Good Ship Grace. There was someone named John D. Jess and the *Chapel of the Air*. When Billy Graham's Hour of Decision was on or when his Crusades were televised, we had to pay attention.

When our family got a television set, there were two Christian programs my parents watched. One was called Challenge: it featured conversations on the great issues of life among a Jewish rabbi, a protestant minister, and a Catholic priest. My father liked Challenge. It was more thought provoking than endless altar calls. My father was a thinker. He was looking for meaning. My mother had meaning nailed down. She wanted comfort.

Another program was called *It Is Written*. It was exceptionally smarmy but I would watch with feigned interest because I knew it impressed my mother. There was a connection between impressing my mother and keeping some unknown terrible thing from happening to me.

Once, after a tedious half hour of *It Is Written*, and in an attempt to align myself with the one thing that mattered to her, I said, "I love God too much!"

She looked at me strangely, unable to negotiate the world of my mind. "You can never love God too much," she said repressively.

When we first got the television set, my mother informed us that it was only for religious or educational programs. That didn't last. Alex and I discovered the Flintstones, Rin Tin Tin, Dennis The Menace. We managed to get them filed under the heading of Wholesome.

The entire family watched Perry Mason and Lawrence Welk —also wholesome—except that the Lennon Sisters had bedroom eyes and Joanne Castle looked like she was having far too much fun at the piano. My mother found the dancers almost unbearable: she could see their underwear. More provocative still was when she *wasn't sure* she could see their underwear.

"I hope she has some pants on." My mother worried excessively about the dancers.

My only memory of my mother being happy was one morning before church when she got word that our house, which was on the market, had a buyer. She had hung up the phone and was putting the Sunday roast in the oven; for an unguarded moment, her worries seem to leave her. Now this was utterly mystifying to me because I had at that point been trying for eight years to make my mother happy and had not, in my estimation, or hers, for that matter, succeeded even once. Then this thing that I did not understand happened, and she was smiling; then we were off to church where she never smiled.

My mother moved us from church to church every time she soured on the pastor. We went to a Covenant Church, an Evangelical Free, a Baptist Church, and a non-denominational Community Church. When packing us up for a new church, her usual indictment was that the pastor had gotten Too Modern. The last move was made not just because the pastor was too modern, but the music was also Too Modern and the women had taken to Wiggling Their Bottoms in an Ungodly Manner when they sang.

Christianity, in our family, equated to getting along with my mother's capricious pronouncements about what God Says. What God said correlated with whatever my mother needed to soothe her anxiety or win an argument. My father was quiet and a bit shy; conflict sucked the life out of him. My mother generated conflict and then stormed into the midst of it and heaved it around just for fun. My parents fought constantly. Once they fought for a week about whether Moses died once or twice. I don't know why this should be a matter of conjecture, but it was the type of thing that could become an issue among people who took the Bible literally. Years later, when I told my therapist my parents had fought over whether Moses died once or twice, he asked "Are you sure they weren't talking about their marriage?" A religious harridan and an alcoholic: this was my parent's marriage. They seemed to make each other miserable and they stayed together for over fifty years.

Soothing the Beast

I CAN NEVER REMEMBER A TIME when I didn't think I was fat and that fat was a bad thing to be. I expect I was anxious about myself long before I started attaching it to the idea of fat.

My mother cramming her breast in my face, declaring, "No alcoholic husband is going to keep me from breast feeding my baby" couldn't have felt good to me. But it soothed my mother; it made her feel like a good mother. Those early experiences of eating for reasons other than pleasure or nutrition hooked comfort and safety with appeasing my mother.

When I was older, appeasement took other forms. My mother loved to entertain and she was famous for her dinner parties. There was always this admonition before any meal that included company: "I want you kids to behave yourselves." No one knew what this entailed, least of all my mother.

At my seventh Thanksgiving, I tried to "behave." I always set the table: "Elena. Would you please set the table? I am in here trying to finish this dinner and the rolls are ruined and it's the least you could do since you are younger than me and you kids could help out once in a while my goodness I do everything for you and you have it so easy and people will be coming in half an hour."

I didn't speak to anyone at the Thanksgiving table. I ate slowly and carefully, and used my napkin to dab at the corners of my mouth. I left my hands in my lap while I chewed. After dinner I heard one of the cousins ask my mother if there was something wrong with me. "Has she been sick?" My mother hadn't noticed.

It took forty years for me to understand what my mother meant by "behave." It meant she did not want to feel anxious. All her anxiety was funneled into one calming mechanism: the kids "behaving." I learned to negotiate her mind at a time when my own brain wiring was forming so our two minds became intertwined. I was a "good" girl to appease my mother and I used food to appease my own anxiety. There was a time when food and mother were the same thing.

When I was away from home, I was anxious about being away from a known source of food. In other people's homes, I was anxious until they offered something to eat, then I worried that it wasn't enough or wasn't what I wanted. I was always worried about something I couldn't name. I had a vague feeling that something awful was going to happen to me. I couldn't verbalize what was worrying me, and even if I could, my mother would have dismissed my concerns: "There's no reason to feel that way." Food was calming if only I didn't have to wait too long for it. I needed it to be available because my mother was not.

There was a home in Bellevue where I didn't worry. Borghild Ringdall went to our church and was a dietitian for the Bellevue public schools. Her house was spacious and clean and always smelled good. She was a large woman, with hair in a braid coiled around the top of her head. She had a thick Norwegian accent that was hard for me to understand. But I understood the stacks of tins and Tupperware containers in the kitchen that were always full of homemade cookies. Mrs. Ringdall was always generous with the cookies and a child never had to wait to get one of each—or two, or five. Her big face beamed down on me when she offered me another.

When my mother baked cookies, she picked out all the best looking ones to give away and save the burnt and crumbled ones for us. "Don't eat the good ones!" she'd yell when she saw us following the scent into the kitchen.

Our afterschool babysitter occasionally baked cookies for my brother and all our friends but I was supposed to be losing weight.

"But I want one, too," I said.

"Well, then go ahead," Eve said, "I don't care if the kids call you Fatty."

We had a babysitter because my mother had Gone Back to Work teaching first grade. In later years, when she was trying to assess what had gone so horribly wrong with her family and why her kids were so "stinking" to her, she traced it back to this: "I should never have Gone Back to Work." Alex always maintained that going back to work had been the best thing she had done for us.

"Can you imagine how we'd have turned out if she'd been there all the time?" he asked darkly.

Food, however, was there all the time. Aside from the burnt and broken cookies, the main junk food in the house was cold cereal: cornflakes and Wheaties. We pleaded to get Trix or Lucky Charms. We finished off those boxes in a matter of days and my mother said,

"I'm not buying any more cold cereal. All you kids do is eat it."

There was always Christmas candy somewhere in the house. My mother bought a lot of it on sale and hid it from me. Then she forgot where it was. Most of the Christmas candy was usually pretty nasty stuff, even when it was fresh: those filled raspberry things and ribbon candy that cut your tongue. But with my focus and tenacity, I could usually uncover just about anything no matter when it was bought or where it was hidden. When there was a putrid smell in my parent's room, I went into the closet like a scent dog to dig out the rotten Easter egg we hadn't found on a hunt.

I worried a lot about my weight. I worried that the communion bread was fattening. It was bread after all; a perfect square half inch of blessed white Wonder bread. When I was 7, I weighed myself on a scale my mother kept in the basement. It said 74. I broke out in a cold sweat. But my father was behind me with his toe pressing on the scale. When he removed his foot, the scale said 62. I felt confused that my father thought this was funny.

In second grade, I wanted to be a crossing guard. I was signed up and had gone through the training. But I took myself off the list when I saw Mary Jane Olsen zipping up the striped orange vest prior to going out for her tour of duty. I was afraid I wouldn't be able to get the vest around me. It looked snug on Mary Jane. I didn't want to risk trying it on. I felt frightened, thinking about how I would be teased.

Visits to the doctor were humiliating because there was always a discussion about my weight while I sat, banging my heels against the examining table and looking out the window.

"I don't know why she keeps gaining weight. We eat fruits and vegetables and cottage cheese. I know. She eats too much bread."

"It's just puppy fat, Mrs. Richmond. It will melt off as she grows."

I thought they were both fools. It wasn't puppy fat and it wasn't going to disappear as I grew.

The growing difficulties with my body might have been mitigated if I had been allowed physical activity. But if there had been a Title IX when I was in school, my mother wouldn't have allowed it in the house. Sports were not ladylike. I could not take ballet lessons because that would give me fat calves. I could not play baseball with the neighborhood kids. My mother raged when my father taught me to pitch and swing a bat. I was not allowed to do hard work. "She's a girl! She's not supposed to lift things!"

My father built a tall swing set with 2 swings. I loved to swing. I memorized Robert Louis Stevenson's poem *The Swing* at an early age and would recite it while I pumped up and down. I could bicycle and play in the woods but that was classified as Being Outdoors. No formal exercise was encouraged.

So I did imaginative, but sedentary things. I read books. I wrote poems and stories. I made mud pies. I organized stuff and made lists just for the fun of it. I played librarian. I learned to embroider. I played the piano and sang.

I played alone. When I was alone, there was no one to criticize me or ignore me. On the other hand, there was no one who took pleasure in me a person, who enjoyed watching me develop, who paid attention to me. I was locked into the airless, anxious cell of my mind with barely enough breathing room for me. My parents were the jailors and there was no one to negotiate my release.

The Grown-Ups

WHEN I WAS FOUR, I learned to read by watching my brother. I stood in front of Alex and watched him read aloud from the Dick and Jane books. As a result, in the beginning I read upside down. My first grade teacher, Miss Wendall, told me I had learned wrong. She put me in the lowest reading group where we looked at pictures until Christmas. So I read books at home—right side up, I was no fool—and endured first grade, watching Miss Wendall sit in reading groups and pick at her pimples.

When I was in second grade, my mother managed to get the cloak of shame removed from, well, mostly her, about my installment in the lowest reading group. She persuaded my teacher, Mrs. Buckman, into administering a test that could ramp me into the top reading group where I belonged. I almost didn't pass the test. I stumbled over the question: Which is louder, a doorbell or a bee?

"A bee," I said

Wrong.

"Well, what if the bee is buzzing in your ear?" I asked.

Mrs. Buckman consulted her manual. "That doesn't matter," she reported.

I thought, "How could it not matter?" It mattered to me because I had been stung by a bee.

Even my mother, who would have aligned herself with me if I had been one of her first graders, asked me worriedly, "Do you really think a bee is louder than a doorbell?"

Mrs. Buckman was her colleague in the district and my mother had hounded her to administer the test so she was exceptionally anxious about the outcome.

There were questions in the test that had many answers but apparently only one of them was right. Here was my great fear meeting me outside the home: something terrible will happen if I don't do the right thing but I can't know ahead of time what that is. I felt trapped with Mrs. Buckman; trapped in a dangerous world with no grown-up on my side.

There was another frightening episode with Mrs. Buckman later that year. The class was finishing lunch. I tossed my milk carton, still half full, into the garbage can. Five minutes later milk was leaking out the bottom and a puddle was forming on the floor.

Mrs. Buckman's loud voice filled the classroom, "Who threw out their milk?" she demanded.

I froze. I looked at the seeping white mass on the floor. I hadn't known that (1) the milk would leak out and (2) it was a capital offense.

Mrs. Buckman quickly counted the number of outstanding milk cartons and told those children they were excused for noon recess. She assembled the rest of us at the crime scene.

"Who is responsible for this?"

I was such a guilt-ridden child that I was continually making amends for imagined crimes and misdemeanors in the closed system that was my inner world. But this was an outside prosecutor and I was terrified at what Mrs. Buckman might do to me if I confessed. Her face was red, spit was coming out the corners of her mouth. All she needed was a fireplace poker and I was back at home. But since all of us were looking uncomfortable, I didn't particularly stand out.

Finally Mrs. Buckman picked a subset of the group being interrogated, and sent them outside. I was one of that group. She must have chosen the kids who she couldn't imagine would do anything so heinous as to throw away their milk so it leaked onto the floor and then *lie* about it. So I escaped.

Another time I was nailed right in the act. Our classroom's toilets were in a short hall connecting us to the other second grade classroom. I had been sitting on the toilet, lost in my own world, singing to myself. When I came out, Mrs. Buckman said, "Were you *singing* in there?"

I blinked, "Yes."

"Don't you know, everyone can *hear* you?"

"I didn't know that was wrong," I said.

"Go sit down," she said.

Something else happened that year, something that became a pivotal memory thirty years later in psycho-therapy. We lived a half mile from Hillaire Elementary and I always walked to and from school. One afternoon, I came home in a downpour and found every window and door in the house standing open and my father at home. I asked him why all the doors and windows were open.

He said, "So you can come in." He looked bleary eyed and smelled funny.

"What are you eating?" I asked him.

"Peanut butter sandwich," he said.

I went into my bedroom. My father followed me in and sat on my bed. "I want to tell you something about your mother," he said. He started to cry. "I just don't want your brother to suffer the way I have suffered," he said.

I stared at him. Suffered. I knew that word from the Bible but I wasn't sure what it meant. I addressed the one thing that made sense to me. "But you don't smell like peanut butter."

I told my mother about it later because I was frightened.

"He said that? He said that about me?" She was indignant but not to be outdone, she added, "You know, he made me cry on our honeymoon."

For years after that, I could never bring myself to say the word *drunk*. My father got "peanut butter," not drunk.

That same year, my mother and I made a shopping trip that provided another piece of fodder for later years: We were at Bellevue Square, which today is a mega mall, but in those days it consisted of Frederick and Nelsons—with a day care room where kids could string macaroni and eat graham crackers while their mothers shopped—a pet store, Petrams Dime Store, J.C. Penneys, and J. J. Newberry. Nearby was a little amusement park. We ran across a vacant lot and at ten cents a ticket, we rode the merry-go-round, Ferris wheel, and roller coaster, or got cotton candy.

On this particular day, I stuck with my mother while we looked at clothes in J.J. Newberry. She wandered along a circular rack, pulling out blouses, holding them up, saying what she liked and didn't like. We moved into the children's clothes. I held up a sweater. "I like this one," I said.

"We don't need that," my mother said and moved on.

In that small moment, a huge part of me shrank through a tiny hole, into a secret place inside of me and pulled a stone over the opening.

I started being unable to sleep at night and I dreaded going to bed. If I managed to fall asleep, I woke up in the night, anxious and afraid. My mother sometimes lay down with me and repeated the words, "Go to sleep toes, relax, toes. Go to sleep feet, relax feet . . ." continuing up to the top of the head. She usually fell asleep herself before she got to the head but I was still wide awake, dreading the time that she would leave. Sometimes I was so persistent in my insomnia that my parents let me sleep with them except what really happened is my father stalked off to my bed and I slept with my mother.

Occasionally I had an experience which I learned had a name when I read about it 45 years later. The book called it a variant of Krakower syndrome. I thought, "Wow, that's that thing that used to happen to me!" I felt like I was floating in a viscous liquid. My hands and feet and limbs were not fully formed and they grew larger and smaller as they came close and then receded in a sack of thick gooey liquid. I found it relaxing and welcomed it because on those nights I could sleep. It suggests to me that life in the womb was a happy experience for me, maybe in part because my mother hoped for a little girl. Even in the womb, I was trying to please my mother. Outside the womb, my air was continually being inhaled right from under my nose by the adults around me.

Aunt Frances

ENTER AUNT FRANCES, the fifth wife of my father's youngest brother. She and my uncle Don, an air traffic controller, lived for many years in Anchorage, Alaska. They came through Seattle once or twice on their way to visit Frances' family in Yazoo City, Mississippi.

Frances was a frothy mint concoction at a table of room temperature water glasses; a lascivious idiom dropped into our prosaic family. I had never seen or heard anything like her in my life. Born in the Mississippi Delta, she had a southern accent that in itself was exotic. She called me Lainie. ("Hell, darlin', it takes too long to say E-Lay-na.")

Her laugh was a wheeze that began deep in her lungs, grew to a Magnolia grandiflora chuckle in the back of her throat and ended with her own private snicker up behind her nose. Sometimes, if her laugh rolled out in a series of uncontrollable waves, she would end up by wiping her eyes saying, "Oh, me," somehow making it come out in four syllables.

She had dark brown hair and smooth skin. She wore lipstick and eye shadow. She winked. I had never known anyone who winked. When Frances winked, her rather small eye would first get huge; by the time the lid came down, she had pulled me into a private secret with her.

She was tall with long, skinny arms and legs. As she aged, her arms and legs stayed slender, and her body got rounder. When she wore flip-flops, her long narrow feet stuck out in front of her like a clown. Sometimes when I see sandpipers running along the ocean beach, I imagine a whole flock of Aunt Franceses.

Don and Frances visited during that awful year of the reading test, the shopping trip and the peanut butter. On their first day with us, Frances and I were playing dress-up. I had on every rope of beads my mother owned, half a dozen brooches—those huge sunburst rhinestone things from the 1950's—earrings, and an old hat of Aunt Ann's. I had lipstick smeared all over my mouth. I was barefoot and my legs and feet were filthy. My mother wanted to take Don and Frances to see the open houses in the Lake Hills housing development that was going on in back of us. She told me to get cleaned up because she wasn't taking me looking like a ragamuffin. But I wasn't planning to shed my finery; besides I thought I looked pretty good.

A fight was building but Frances took my hand and said, "Let her be, Mary. Everyone can think she's my little girl."

I could do no wrong around Frances. She laughed when I was being funny and took me seriously when I wasn't. She had a train load of nieces and nephews but she made me feel like I was the only one. I was adrift among the alienated Richmonds and Frances pulled me to her. When my mother criticized me, Frances gave her a look that said "Don't start with *me*, Mary." In my inner world, Frances and my mother were Churchill and Hitler. When she and Don visited us at the red house in Bellevue, the war had only just begun.

A Musical Education

IN THE FINAL UPHEAVAL OF THAT TUMULTUOUS seventh year of my life, we moved from Bellevue to Olympia. My father was an accountant in the Washington state health department, whose offices moved from Seattle to the state capital in the early 1960s. Our family's move was accomplished with uncharacteristic smoothness as far as I was aware. In early June, my mother took Alex and me to Montana to visit her family. When we returned, it was to a new house in Olympia.

My father was not along on the Montana trip. We didn't do well on family vacations. The four of us in a car was a combustible mix, no matter the distance we were going. Once we set out for a weekend trip to Victoria B.C., driving from Bellevue to Anacortes to take the ferry through the San Juan Islands. We pulled up to the ferry docks just as a ferry was leaving. There would be other ferries that day but my mother was beside herself.

"If you didn't take so long steaming your face and primping in the bathroom, we wouldn't have missed the ferry!" she yelled at my father.

My father silently turned the car around and drove us all the way back home without saying a word. That was the end of the trip to Victoria.

We returned from Montana to an old house in Olympia and a freshly dried out father. His drinking had stopped, we all attended the Tumwater Evangelical Free Church, and the family had entered its golden age, at least by my mother's estimation. We were all saved from hell but nobody was happy on earth. We ticked along like that for years.

With alcohol no longer a major preoccupation, something bloomed in my father and he became a great enthusiast of classical music, especially opera, which wedged open a tiny door in our strained relationship. He listened to Wagner for hours. He walked around singing the motifs. I learned to recognize Siegfried, the curse, the sword, the Rheingold, the Valkyrie and Valhalla. Occasionally he would play the Valhalla motif on the piano, and then the first line of the Chopin military polonaise.

Occasionally my mother had her own cultural eruption and sat down to play her repertoire: "O Christmas Tree" and "Jesus Loves Me." I don't know what precipitated it but then I never knew what precipitated anything with my mother.

Both my parents were supportive of music lessons. Alex and I began learning piano in Bellevue and neither of us had missed a lesson in two years until the trip to Montana. Once in Olympia, we were in piano lessons before we were in our new school.

I had learned to play the piano the same way I had learned to read: I watched my brother. Alex practiced "C-D-E, make a boat, round and round and round it floats" in his Leila Fletcher Piano Course Book One, the orange book. I looked at the written music and saw what Alex's fingers were doing. I tried it and never looked back. I started formal lessons when I was four.

We practiced on a 1903 upright Haddorf piano that had belonged to my grandmother, Louise Knott, and had been used for a time in the Whitman College conservatory in Walla Walla. The piano's beautiful soul lived in a plain, sturdy cabinet. It was to stay with me into my adult years.

We took piano lessons at the Lavinia Jennings Music Studio, which was located in the front room of Lavinia Jennings house. I always rang the bell to enter Lavinia Jennings Music Studio; every other music teacher who taught music in her home has told me to walk in. I rang the bell and heard the thump, thump, thump of her brown pumps as she came to open the door, dressed to the nines in one of two different teaching outfits.

One was a double-breasted green jumper worn with a frilly white blouse buttoned up to her chin, the other was a straight brown skirt and plain white blouse opened to her supra-sternal notch with a tiny cross supervising its eroticism. It was her hair, however, that fascinated. I had not yet seen the movie Gone With the Wind, but Mrs. Jennings' hair gave me a reference point for both Scarlett O'Hara and Miss Pittypat. It was a birthday cake of curls piled a foot high with masses of bobby pins sticking out like candles. Every week I checked to see if any bobby pins were about to spring loose.

I sat in her dining room and looked at the one book available for waiting students, a cartoon book called *Misery Loves Company*. When I used the bathroom, I sneaked a look at other parts of the house. The kitchen gleamed with clean. There was a guest bedroom and an enticing staircase to the upstairs. I longed to see what was upstairs.

Once when I was in the bathroom, I noticed the medicine cabinet was open a crack. I pulled it a few inches further to get a better look at the riot inside. The door made a loud cranky sound.

"Elena." Thump thump thump. Mrs. Jennings rounded the corner and bumped into me shooting out of the bathroom. "What are you doing in the medicine cabinet?"

"Nothing," I looked straight at her and said honestly, "It was already open."

She closed the medicine cabinet firmly and followed me out to the front room.

When it was time for my lesson, Mrs. Jennings handed me the fountain pen she kept in a pen holder on the edge of the piano. I signed and dated my page in her ledger. By the end of each year, I had written my name 40 times, line after line.

When it came round to my first recital with Mrs. Jennings, she told me it would be held in the studio.

"Where is the studio?" I looked around. I thought it was in her back yard or maybe in town somewhere.

Mrs. Jennings looked at me as though I had suddenly become half-witted. "Right here." she said. "This is the studio."

"But it's your front room."

"It's. The. Studio."

In early spring, a stack of sheet music two inches thick sat on her piano. Mrs. Jennings selected two pieces for me to play in the spring recital. I never had a choice about what I played and I hated the recital music.

About a month before the recital, Mrs. Jennings asked the girls for the color of their dresses and she meticulously made note. The day of the recital, we went into the guest bedroom to find a big box of white boutonnières for the boys and colorful corsages to match the girl's dresses. In the world of small town children's piano recitals, the corsages were a classy note.

On the day of the recital, the performers sat in the order listed on the program, twenty of us lined up as though to be shot. We sat in Mrs. Jennings' impeccable kitchen—as far as I could tell, she and her husband, Sumner, never ate actual food—and sweated out the wait for our performance. I desperately wanted something in my mouth but I had never so much as smelled dinner cooking or seen the remains of breakfast in this house. Only once was there a bowl of shining green apples, but they turned out to be wax.

The parents sat on rows of folding chairs in the front room. While the house heaved with sweat and nerves, my father occupied himself by writing comments in the margins of the programs, critiquing the performances. My mother kept her knees together and monitored who was and wasn't doing the same.

Mrs. Jennings was the pianist in a rollicking Pentecostal denomination where members who are "slain in the spirit" lie down on the floor and speak in tongues. While as far as I could make out, she went through life with a stick up her butt, she must have taken it out when she went to church. Literally on the way to church because when the car backed out of the driveway, she was still sitting ramrod straight, next to, but not touching Sumner. At the piano, playing those old gospel songs, she must have rocked.

Mrs. Jennings taught both Alex and me how to chord, if not to rock. For my money, there is no better way to learn music theory. She worked from the church hymnal and taught us how to know what chords were being used in the harmonization. We started with simple hymns that only had three chords and progressed to ones that used the relative minors, diminished chords, modulations, and more exotic harmonies. She dragged the end of her fountain pen—the same one we signed in with–down the index of the hymnal, looking for the keys she wanted. She knew the key of every hymn. I watched the pen rub up and down the index, making little squeaky sounds that sent tingles down my spine and calmed me.

She showed us how to play "bass, chord, bass, chord." We learned how to do little runs and honky-tonk touches, but nothing too sexy. Alex was better at it than I was because he had a good ear. He made the piano say funny things. He played "At Calvary" with flourishes that made even my mother smile. I watched the back of his ears as he played; they moved up and down when he grinned with pleasure at the attention. There wasn't a lot that made him happy.

We were both unhappy and music was solace. Alex messed around at the piano in a world of sound, and I was a collector of songs. I learned songs by picking the notes out on the piano, fitting the words to the notes and accompanying my own singing. I learned all the folksongs in four books of Mark Nevin's *Tunes You Like* and sang them to myself.

I changed piano teachers when I was in junior high. Jane Page was a widow with a small child. I wouldn't have known that she had other income besides her teaching such as life insurance and an Army wife's pension. When I made a decision later in life to make my living teaching private music lessons, it never occurred to me that it couldn't be done.

I stayed with Jane all through high school. She encouraged me to teach and took me to conventions of the Washington State Music Teachers Association.

She introduced me to Bach and I discovered his calming powers. I played most of the inventions and a few of the fugues. When I sat at the piano and wound my way through a Bach invention, I felt safe from the family chaos. The music seemed to come from someplace where it was already living a life that it didn't need me to support. It traveled into me as I played the notes, picked me up and carried me through all its circumnavigations to its reassuring conclusions. It was enormously comforting.

Alex and I both escaped into music but our escape routes didn't often intersect. When they did it was as a result of my father's influence. We didn't care for Wagner or my mother's Christian radio but my father had a few records. One was Marty Robbins' Gunfighter ballads. We knew all the words to those songs: El Paso, Cool Water, Strawberry Roan. My brother and I went around the house singing "with a big iron on his chest!" at the top of our lungs. We did the same with the songs on old 78 records. We sang "The railroad runs through the middle of the house." We had long discussions about how that would work exactly. We made diagrams. Bing Crosby singing "Pistol Packin' Mama" inspired us to periodically yell: "Lay that thing down before it goes off and hurts somebody!"

We had an old wind-up Victrola in our basement with records a quarter inch thick. Mostly they were marches and classical recordings, but there were also some World War One songs. My favorite was "K-K-

K-Katy." We cleared out a course through the basement and garage, buckled on our roller skates, cranked up the Victrola, and skated for hours.

My father gave me a record player on my 13th Christmas, the year I opened every present under the tree to see what was inside. Not just the ones addressed to me, mind you, but every last one. Then I carefully rewrapped them. It was a useful experiment. It satisfied my excruciating curiosity but it ruined that Christmas Eve so I never needed to do it again.

My parents had gotten into a huge fight about the record player. My mother didn't want me to have one, principally, I think, because I wanted one. Since she wouldn't sign on, my father bought it for me without telling her. I played Broadway soundtracks that I checked out of the public library and the Monkees albums, which I was finally allowed to buy because at least they weren't the Beatles.

My father also came through for me when I wanted a guitar. My mother didn't want me playing a guitar because that led to other things about which she was vague, but drugs and prostitution were the least of it. She allowed that I could have a mandolin but not a guitar. The reasoning behind this was that her favorite brother, Alec, had played a mandolin.

Alec knew songs and dances from the old country; he played the fiddle, the mandolin and the harmonica. He had also been a great womanizer, a belligerent drunk, and had died while he was in his early 40s from a gunshot wound during an alcoholic binge with his buddies. This I learned much later in life from my cousins. My mother told me that Alec had been murdered by people who were jealous of his talents. She idolized Alec; when she idolized someone, they became exactly who she needed them to be. Thus it was that my mother insisted Beverly Sills was a born again Christian.

"She's Jewish, Mom."

"God understands these things. He makes allowances"

"What does that mean?"

"What did you do with that red jacket I made you?" My mother had a black belt in non-sequiturs.

I had already had three years of violin lessons because of Uncle Alec. I had learned to play on his violin. Our beagles, Colonel and Cuddles, sat side by side on the porch next to my bedroom window and howled when I practiced. They wouldn't go to the other side of the house; they just took their positions and howled. When I started private violin lessons, the teacher did more or less the same thing. She covered her ears and said, "It's flat! It hurts! Can't you hear that?" I didn't much care for playing the violin.

And so I got a mandolin, which I then learned how to play with the help of a Mel Bay book. But the next Christmas, my father gave me a guitar. There was a lady named Laura Weber on PBS television out of San Francisco who taught a series of folk guitar lessons. I sat in front of the television with my guitar and absorbed Series One, Two, and Three three times in a row over the course of a year and a half. I was so engaged with Laura Weber that when she rhetorically asked "Are you ready?" I answered "Yes." I learned guitar. I learned to play and sing along, do a few bits of fancy work, a variety of strums and never progressed beyond Series Three but played the guitar for the next 40 years. I sold the mandolin at a yard sale.

Coming Sick

I GOT MY FIRST PERIOD AT AGE 13. Seeing the blood on the toilet paper, I yelled, "MOM!"

She came busting into the bathroom. "Oh dear," she said. "It's started."

Fortunately the school nurse had forewarned me what It was. My mother never talked about menstruation with me. Now that it could be spoken of, she called it Come Sick.

"Did you Come Sick?" she would ask me.

"No," I would say pointedly. "I'm. Having. My. Period."

During the 60s there were two kinds of sanitary napkins: Moddess and Kotex. My mother used Moddess. She didn't approve of Kotex. I think it had something to do with the women in their advertisements. They looked happy and, because of this, cheap. Moddess had mature, unsmiling women on their boxes and they made industrial size sanitary napkins. My mother used Moddess, so they were good enough for me, too. None of those tiny Kotex things for girls. She felt the same way about bras. Most of my friends wore wearing training bras, but I got outfitted with something For Support.

The only thing my mother actually said to me about Coming Sick was that tampons were for married women and that I was never to broach the topic of *menstruation* around a male. It should barely even be discussed among women. She grew red in the face, propounding this to me.

She needn't have worried because there weren't any boys. I was pudgy, awkward, and smart. I had a few male friends in high school, ones who were as uncertain of themselves as I was. Eric Monson and I ate lunch together and messed around on the guitar. Once we kissed swiftly, unexpectedly. Then it was over and we never spoke of it or did it again. We were lab partners in biology. I had a great deal of natural curiosity but it didn't lead to an interest in science. Every time I looked in the microscope, no matter whether it was a drop of liquid or a blade of grass, I saw thick black lines criss-crossing my view and I disinterestedly drew them.

"What are those?" Mr. Kendrick asked.

"It's what I saw."

He looked in the microscope. "Well, look again."

Somehow I realized I was seeing my own eyelashes, which were unusually long and thick and slanted down across my eyes.

"Don't hold your eyes that way," my mother said of my luscious lashes. "It looks Come Hither."

My mother's advice to me, as I grew up, wasn't for me or about me. She was living in another world: "Don't let anyone stick a needle in your arm." In Olympia, Washington. In 1969. Years later, I realized she was thinking about the white slave trade of the 1920s, something she might have heard about when she was a young girl off the farm and going to high school in Miles City, Montana. She consulted the phantoms in her mind and then advised me.

Alex and I listened to Bob Dylan records in his bedroom sometimes. We managed détentes when music was involved. One night, I was getting sleepy so I slipped out to get ready for bed, and then popped back in to hear one more track. My mother caught up to me on my way back to my bed.

"Did you change into your nightgown in front of your brother?" she demanded.

I stared at her. What on earth was that about?

She might have been more concerned about a game Alex and I played when we were small. We faced each other from opposite ends of the sofa, with pillows protecting our crotches. We took turns ramming our feet into each other's pillow, feeling the genital stimulation. I always assumed that no parent saw us because no one told us to stop. At some point, we just did. That game with Alex was as sexually adventurous as I got until I was in my thirties.

My mother issued other mysterious warnings: "Always wear your nightgown to bed because"—staged whispered—"your dad might come in and look at you."

The only usable advice my mother gave me about sex and men were the times she said, "Why don't you ask Frances about that?" It's a tribute to my Aunt Frances' magic that my mother didn't view her as competition. I was even allowed to visit her during that thirteenth summer.

Don and Frances had by then moved from Anchorage to Albuquerque, and Frances had collected a passel of her nieces and nephews from Mississippi to spend the summer with her.

It was my first time in an airplane. The plane was late leaving Seattle so I missed the connector flight in Los Angeles. For my troubles, I was upgraded to first class and was watched over, not only by the stewardesses, as they were then called, but by the woman next to me on the plane who I remember as the kindest and most beautifully dressed woman I had ever seen. Unbeknownst to me, I was also being watched over by my air traffic controller uncle in Albuquerque who was beside himself that I had missed my connection and was at large in LAX.

By the time I flew into Albuquerque at around midnight, Frances, her mother, whom everyone called Granny, Ronny Neal, Kenny, and Debbie Lou had been out to the airport three times to meet every plane coming in from Los Angeles. They were in high spirits and excited to meet me.

"Your uncle Don threw a hissy fit when you missed your flight, Lainie," Frances said. "It sure is nice to see you, darlin'."

I felt like a celebrity.

Everyone had been given a summer nickname: "Hee Haw Debbie Lou-pee-in-her-shoe," "Kenny Tiddybaby;" I forget Ronnie's nickname but he was homesick and went back to Mississippi the next day. I looked at Aunt Frances to see if she approved of the names.

"Hell, Lainie," Debbie said to me, "They were her idea." Debbie was younger than I was and she got to say "hell."

I stayed for three weeks. It was hot and humid; there was no air conditioning and all the doors and windows of my aunt's house stood open. We all wore fewer clothes than I had ever been allowed to wear. Frances moved through the house, dragging on her cigarette, an iced tea in her other hand, saying, "Damn, it's hot" fifty times a day.

The southern kids were funny and likable. I had never been around such freedom.

"Kenneth Edward Tidwell, you get your butt in here and give me back that book!"

"Lainie said I could see it first."

"The hell she did!"

Frances charged out of the kitchen waving a spoon. "You-all hush up your mouths or I'll beat your arses in! Granny's tryin' to nap!"

Granny appeared in the doorway, "Lord, Frances, I couldn't sleep with this racket."

"Now, Lainie, you-all sit on the couch with Mother and let her get to know you. The rest of you, go fight in the street."

I sat down awkwardly.

"Frances," said Granny. "I don't think this child knows what to call me." She looked at me. "Hell, darlin', I'm just Granny Grunt." So that was *her* nickname.

My personality expanded in the warmth of a month with Frances and company. Then my parents and brother arrived by car.

Frances took my family sightseeing. At the Pueblo Indian reservation, she took pictures of us with an instant Polaroid camera. She clowned and laughed behind the camera and snapped the four of us, standing uncomfortably on the edge of a fun family vacation.

My mother looked at one of snapshots. "I look fat," she complained.

Frances laughed, "Well, you are fat, Mary!"

I looked at Frances in astonishment and then at my mother to see how this would play. No one talked to my mother like that.

My mother laughed. Her face relaxed. For a few seconds, she looked like a person someone might want to know.

My family drove back to Seattle via California, stopping one evening for dinner in Pismo Beach. We were seated at a lovely table with china and sparkling crystal and finger bowls—I'll never forget the finger bowls. I was enjoying the swank and a new sense of myself when my father said to my mother, not bothering to lower his voice, "Can't you do something so she doesn't stick out so much?" Something inside me did indeed come sick and I hunched below the table.

The Undifferentiated Ego Mass

"BUT *YOU COULD NOT HAVE A GREEN ROSE. BUT PERHAPS SOMEWHERE* IN THE WORLD YOU COULD."

James Joyce's *A Portrait of the Artist as a Young Man* made a huge impression on me when I was in high school. I made green roses out of tissue paper, gave one to my English teacher and kept one for me. Later I took mine to college and kept it for years until the green was dusty and faded.

The green rose had the same symbolic power as the "stars of the morning" in the little Sunday school song of a dozen years earlier. Somewhere there was something that I needed; it wasn't here and it wasn't available now. Like Stephen Daedalus, I had some notion that I belonged somewhere, that somewhere I was loved; I just hadn't discovered where that was. I had a desire to be free of my mother but I needed something from her that would enable me to leave. I needed her to willingly let go so I could breathe my own air. I couldn't imagine how that was going to happen.

Generally speaking, that's something fathers are for: they help you leave home and establish yourself. My father and I made a nascent connection with each other through an appreciation of classical music: his interest in opera had spread from Wagner to bel canto. I had started formal voice lessons and was learning classical vocal singing. Music was one thing we shared, but inevitably we also aligned with each other against my mother's repressive and unimaginative religious beliefs.

By this time, my mother was on her own with religion. She went to church several times a week and joined every Bible study and women's group she could cram into her schedule. My father stopped going altogether. He weakened the supremacy of Billy Graham, who was like the Pope in our house, by pointing out that in his ministry, once you were saved, there wasn't a heck of a lot of new material and he was, frankly, bored by it. Beyond C.S. Lewis, he didn't find anything in evangelical Christianity that stimulated him intellectually. He was a searcher, my father. I believe that he hoped to think and reflect his way out of the underlying depression that had not disappeared when he stopped drinking. He decided that Christianity did not fill the empty places.

I rode his coat-tails and stopped going to church, as well. I was sick to death of religion and of my mother.

"Aren't you going to church?" she demanded of me.

"No, I'm not."

She turned to my father. "You should set an example."

"I am setting an example," He said. "I'm staying home."

"Well, Elena needs to be at church. You should put your foot down and make her go."

My father theatrically stamped one foot. This was my mother's cue to head for the garage with a siren of warnings, threats and declarations about God's will. My father once explained the Doppler effect as my mother walking through the house, past wherever he was sitting, trying to read, and out the door, talking the entire time.

Instead of going to church, my father read William James, Freud, Plato, Newton, and Shakespeare—the dudes in the Great Books of the Western World. While my mother was at church, or reading her Bible or watching The Billy Graham Hour of Decision, he and I sat in his den and talked about the Great Books. Every now and again she would burst into the room, look at us sitting across the room from each other, and want to know what we were talking about. If we were laughing, she assumed the joke was about her—often it was—and she took silent offense.

My mother later told me that during my last two years of high school, when my brother was gone and she was home with my father and me, she thought she was going crazy. I was curious about her baseline for measuring crazy. She went for long periods of time not speaking to us.

She shut herself into her bedroom—my parents had separate bedrooms at this point—and read her Bible, which gave her no reference point with which to understand what was happening to her marriage or to her relationship with me.

She came home with a new hairdo and with eye makeup, something I had never seen her wear, after a makeover at the Mode O' Day beauty salon. She looked fabulous, like someone in a magazine. She also looked painfully uncomfortable, walked passed my father's compliments, went straight to the bathroom, got in the shower and washed everything off.

One morning, she fainted. There was a huge thump in the kitchen. When my father went to investigate, he found my mother on the floor. He gathered her up and carried her to the couch, his face full of alarm and tenderness. When she came to, he bustled off to get her some water and a blanket.

My mother clutched at me, "Was my nightgown up? Did your dad see me?"

I stared at her. I didn't understand either of these incidents. I didn't want to know things about their marriage.

I had my first job by then: teaching piano. I had ten students. I took my earned money along with some fabric and patterns to Sandra, the mother of a friend, and asked her to make me some clothes that fit. My mother had been trying to dress me all my life but had yet to make me anything I wanted to wear. Or that was even ready to wear. She whipped up A-line things in hideous cotton prints, threw them at me with all the seams edges hanging out, no buttons, no hem, and said,

"There. That's done. You can finish it."

I didn't want to finish it and I wasn't going to wear it. But I was resigned to knowing she would rather walk naked down Capitol Boulevard than buy actual clothes. She even made underwear. So I made lists of the colors I liked, and picked out fabric and patterns.

I gave her a tape measure and said, "Here. Measure me. You keep saying I have a short waist."

Thus I proved to her that I knew standard patterns could be taken up a half inch in the waist so they would fit me. But my mother had known all along that bodies came in different shapes. What she didn't want to know was that I was a separate entity from her. She made me a dress with a pattern and fabric I had chosen but she yanked the waist up 2 inches.

"There. I shortened the waist. Are you satisfied?"

The dress was ruined, and I was in tears.

"If you would just lose a little weight, maybe you wouldn't be so short waisted."

Sandra measured my body without making comments about my size and made me some royal blue culottes and a dark gold jacket, every seam tacked flat and every thread snipped. They fit perfectly.

My mother phoned Sandra and demanded, "Why does my daughter hate me?"

I was mortified. God how I wished she would be of some help to me, or at least stop squeezing the life out of me. I hated her.

I aligned myself with my father. We had a little cabal, just the two of us. I had a pet name for him: I called him Arthur, the remnant of an elaborate—and very boring—joke. He called me E-Pooh. We stayed up late watching Roller Derby on Saturday nights. We went to the opera in Seattle. We dated. I loved being with him. He was charming and funny. I felt happy and stimulated. I was getting some species of attention.

But it was a terrible choice I had to make: to wrench my mother's hold on me, I had to move towards a man who needed a mother as much as I did and who expressed his neediness as though I was already an adult. I had to constrict the memory of his sitting on my bed, drunk, when I was seven. I had to figure out how to breathe around his remark about my breasts. I had to think around my mother's earlier warnings that he might come to my room to look at me if I didn't wear a nightgown to bed. Both parents impinged on the space that should have been reserved for my young fantasies about feeling attractive and desirable. Instead of thinking about sex and flirtation playfully, I saw it as a deadly serious game.

Even so, Arthur was more fun than my mother. Our camaraderie for a time helped me begin to find a fragile identity of my own. Arthur enjoyed my adoration. He felt vindicated for, what was it? "How much he had suffered." My mother read her Bible, prayed, and sighed. In her own way, she also felt vindicated. The role of the martyr suited her. And whatever the competition going on between my mother and me, I had, temporarily, won.

Awake, My Soul

IN THE MIDST OF MY FAMILY'S DOMESTIC CONFUSION, I had the best year I would have for a long time. I lost 35 pounds without even thinking about it. My appetite moved from food to other attractions. The voice lessons were working a magic in me. My body, which had been denied physical activity all its life on the grounds that it wasn't ladylike, loved the feeling of singing.

The entire body expands in singing. You bring everything you've got into the breath. In one phrase, you can use up all your air, think your life is over, and find out that there's more where that came from; more breath than you dreamed possible. It rushes through the throat and reverberates in your head. To sing was to feel alive.

I loved everything about classical vocal music: the old Italian songs one learns at the beginning of voice training, the exercise books like Concone and Vaccai, the original teachers of bel canto. I sang "Tu Lo Sai" and won a first in a regional music contest. I sang "O Mio Babbino Caro" from *Gianni Schicchi* and "Deh vieni non tardar" from *The Marriage of Figaro*.

My singing apex in high school was to learn "Lucy's aria" from *The Telephone* and perform it in a recital that took place in my teacher Pat Jacob's studio. My encore was "Adelaide's Lament" from *Guys and Dolls*. When I sniffed loudly and blew my nose as part of the act, I heard my mother gasp, "Oh, Elena!" laugh nervously and say to someone—except that we all heard—"I didn't know she was going to do that!"

In spite of my mother's outburst, I remember that evening fondly. Pat was gracious and proud. I basked in her love and appreciation of me while my mother ran around telling everyone how she had started me in piano lessons when I was 4.

I was in drama that year. I felt normal within the drama crowd, ever the folks from the island of misfit toys. With my weight loss, I looked good enough to have landed the ingénue role in *Dinny and the Witches*, the spring play. I had a scene in a wedding dress. In another scene I got to rip off that wedding dress to reveal hot pants and black tights. I danced a seductive dance that Todd Carroll had choreographed and taught me. It was the most fun I had ever had in my life. For 2 weeks, Todd was my boyfriend, which meant he appeared at my side when I arrived on campus, and followed me around, and we kissed a lot. And then it just stopped.

Arthur came to all three performances of the play and reportedly, his face lit up with pleasure when I did my dance. This news flash from my drama teacher made me extremely uncomfortable. As long as I was sitting across the room from him, talking, that was one thing. But the idea of him noticing my body frightened me. He might come to my bed at night and look at me…He got pleasure out of seeing me dancing in hot pants…He thinks I stick out too much. The images formed a large hard mass in my mind and sat there, undigested, obstructing the flow of everything else.

After my successful year of singing and performing, I formed a different kind of hard mass: a vocal nodule. I was practicing too much for a young voice, and trying difficult music like "Un bel dì" from Madame Butterfly, all unbeknownst to my voice teacher.

The vocal nodule stopped the sound from coming out. It impinged on my vocal cords so they couldn't vibrate when the air came through. The only cure was to stop singing—stop talking even—for months. I was shocked. I cried for weeks, and the low grade depression that had always been with me, deepened.

Everyone was optimistic that after a rest cure, I'd be singing again. But six months later when the doctor pronounced the nodule gone, there was still no sound coming out. I had lost all my high notes. My teacher didn't understand vocal strain nor did she seem to understand how heartbroken I was. No one could explain or understand why I didn't have my voice back when there was nothing medically wrong with my vocal cords. It would be a long time before I found my voice and before I understood why I had lost it.

In the meantime, I lost my confidence. I was frightened. Nothing in life thus far had given me greater joy than singing. Because my parents were supportive of my musical abilities, I had developed an idea that singing was a way to become extraordinary and from that, to feel loved. Deeper down, I believed that God had taken my voice away from me because of how much I loved to sing. But deeper still, in my subterranean sexuality, the vocal nodule effectively got my body off the stage where my father might look at it.

My mother started asking "Why don't you sing anymore?"

I said, "Weren't you there? I got a vocal nodule."

It seemed to be all of a piece with our home life. No one wanted anything to be wrong and if something was wrong, no one wanted to think about why that was. I got more depressed and food began to be a comfort again. My mother, to her credit, communicated concern for me and not for the way I reflected on her.

I fathomed her concern when she came out with one of her non-sequiteurs: "Mrs. Pucelle is worried about you. She says you never have friends with you and you ate a quart of ice cream all by yourself."

Mrs. Pucelle came every other week to clean the house. When I came home from school just as she was about to wash the kitchen floor, I loaded up with everything I could find to eat and closed myself into my bedroom. I felt anxious about food being inaccessible for the time it would take the floor to dry.

I was stuck in a big lump with my parents at a time I needed them to sort out what was going on among the three of us. Arthur was helplessly silent. And my mother put as much psychic distance as she could put between herself and me. She managed to insert the cleaning lady who came every other week.

My senior year I spent a lot of time alone reading Tolstoy and Michener, chewing bubble gum cigars and riding my bike. I lived at the public library. Small town Carnegie Libraries in the 1960s were womb-like places. Even the smell was, well, enclosed.

I liked to station myself a few feet from someone who was browsing in fiction and listen to the sound of a finger running along the spines of books; the crinkle of the cellophane covers when a book was opened, the tap of a book being replaced on the shelf. Little fingers of pleasure traveled up and down my spine and I got a buzz of contentment and relaxation. Every so often, so as not to blow my cover, I picked up a book and pretended to read the dust jacket. Truthfully, I couldn't have made out two words during those little spells because I was in a kind of hypnotic state.

At the library, I could check out a load of books, read them or not read them, take them all back the next day and do it again; and no one yelled at me for being wasteful, lazy, or whatever was the indictment du jour. If I was curious about something not in the stacks themselves, the reference librarian salivated at the prospect of a good sleuth. She found books and articles for me on interlibrary loan. Something could come in from Delaware just for me. I could look at it for two minutes, decide it wasn't what I expected and put it on the returns desk. The point is, there was plenty of stuff in the library just waiting to be used, and it was available to me. It was everything that home wasn't.

Narrow Escapes

I SPENT THE SUMMER AFTER I GRADUATED from high school in a little Kentucky mountain town. Having read Catherine Marshall's book, *Christy*, half a dozen times, my head was full of romantic ideas about the mountains. I wanted to hear old English ballads that had found their way to the Appalachians. I was going to sit on porches in the hollows and listen to singers sing the old songs. It didn't quite work out that way because Nashville had permeated all the outposts. I did sit on porches, though, and met a lot of friendly folks who treated me like royalty.

I arranged my summer in Kentucky all on my own. I was to work with a minister setting up vacation Bible schools. VBS was another dreadful phenomenon of Evangelical Christianity, except for the part where you got to make stuff with paper mâché, Popsicle sticks, pipe cleaners, macaroni, and huge pasty gobs of Elmer's glue all over everything. I managed to get the gig even though at that point, I wouldn't have called myself a Christian. I was cynical enough to think that it hardly mattered. I knew a lot of songs, mostly didn't mind the religious ones if they had decent tunes, and I could fake the rest. In general, "faking it" was turning into a good coping strategy for me.

I wrote letters, made all the arrangements and announced to my parents that I needed the plane fare. My father received all this with his usual bemusement—he hadn't even *had* parents, so he didn't know what parents did with nearly grown up children. But my mother put up a fuss. She called Kentucky to make sure I was going to stay with decent folks and not some weirdos.

When she decided it would be okay, she added darkly, "It's not *my* idea to go traipsing off all over the country."

My plane from Seattle to Lexington left at midnight. The airport was creepy at that time of night. I went to the ladies room. Sitting in the stall, I looked up at the sound of a noise. A man was hanging over the edge of the divider, trying to reach my purse on the door hook. I yelled, "You get outta here!" as loud as I could, surprising myself. He disappeared.

I was trembling when I got back to where my parents were waiting, but I didn't say anything. I thought they wouldn't let me go if reminded of the sort of thing that can happen to someone who goes traipsing off by herself. I had a vague notion that it was somehow my fault that the man had followed me into the ladies room. ("It's the way you walk, Elena, it means you Want Something," or "Don't hold your eyes that way, it attracts the Wrong Kind of Man.") I knew that my parents would have nothing calming to say, so I kept it to myself.

When I came back from the summer, I told my mother about the experience. She said smugly, "I knew something was wrong when you came out of the rest room."

I stared at her. Why was everything always about her?

"Why are you looking at me?" she asked. "I did know something was wrong."

"I am so happy for you," I said.

I enjoyed my summer in the Appalachians, even if I didn't hear any Child ballads. I was 18 years old and was given more responsibility than seems advisable when I think about it now. I lived with the pastor and his wife and drove their VW bus on mountain roads all over the county, sometimes alone, sometimes with a load of children. When we took a group of kids to Memphis, I drove the van.

When I was driving alone, I got in the habit of stopping at a vista point, a cliff's edge known as Widow's Branch. One day I decided to take a photo. I set the handbrake and got out. As I was steadying the camera, I felt the van start to move past me toward the cliff's edge. I grabbed the door handle in an attempt to physically hold it back. When that, of course, didn't work, I yanked open the door and stuck my foot on the brake pedal. I crawled carefully in, reversed the van, and drove home shaking.

I didn't say anything about my near death experience to anyone for years. Most immediately, I was afraid my car keys would be taken away. By now it was my habit to keep things to myself. Nearly 40 years later, I occasionally revisit that moment in dreams and I still frighten myself awake.

I taught private piano students and guitar classes. I had made up my own lesson plans from my two years of watching Laura Weber on PBS. But best of all were the big sing-alongs with the children. We sang "This Land," and "The Ants Go Marching." They taught me "The Other Day I Met a Bear," and "My hand on myself, what is this here?" I taught them "Pick a Little, Talk a Little" from *The Music Man*, and "The Ugly Bug Ball" from *Summer Magic*, "All Night, All Day," "Jennie Jenkins," and "Tzena Tzena."

Richard was a frequent visitor to the manse when I was there. I thought he was coming to talk theology with the pastor, since he was down from Harvard to do an internship at a church in one of the valleys. One night I excused myself shortly after he arrived and went upstairs to my room.

The pastor's wife followed me a few minutes later. "Don't you know Richard is coming to see you?" she asked.

"He is?" I was surprised, and not pleasantly. I didn't know whether or not I wanted to see Richard. I didn't know whether or not it mattered what I wanted.

I ended up seeing a lot of Richard that summer but I'm not sure he saw much of me. I remember him being impressed that I had read William James' *The Varieties of Religious Experience*. This put me in a dilemma. I knew I could have a deeper experience of spirituality than evangelical Christianity would ever give me and the book title alone gave me a place to begin. I could see that it was an impressive read for a high school student. But the truth was I had not understood much of the book.

I was precocious, another way of saying "faking it." My mind had always tried to take me places the rest of me couldn't go. As a child, a few months after I had figured out how to play the piano, I thought, "If this is all that's involved, I can play anything!" When I dug out Chopin's military polonaise and tried to match the notes with the keys, I learned that there was something more complicated going on.

Something complicated was going on with me in regards to Richard. He came over a lot. I stopped disappearing into my room because everyone expected me to welcome the attention. My mother, back in Olympia, whom I didn't have enough sense to keep out of the loop, bombarded me with questions. I understood that A Man was Attracted to Me and I was expected to welcome him. My social skills were just barely enough to ride out my confusion and fear. When I was with Richard, I had a strange feeling that there were two of me. There was me who pretended to have fun, who acted like Richard was interesting, and who had read William James at the age of 18. Then there was me who was confused about why this didn't feel good at all when everyone else seemed to be giddy about it.

I wanted a relationship with a man, but it was my understanding that romance felt good. Being with Richard didn't feel good and I didn't understand why. When I went back to Seattle at the end of the summer, I hoped that would be the end of it. But Richard was to surface again later.

Walla Walla

I RETURNED FROM KENTUCKY IN TIME to head off to my first year of college in Walla Walla, Washington. My father's family had been associated with Walla Walla and with Whitman College from its early inception as an academy. Some of the greats and all my uncles had attended. My father had graduated in 1932 with a degree in economics. When I was a child, he explained his work as an auditor: "I sit around all day adding up the number of candy bars I eat." Now there's a Whitman education being well used.

I never seriously thought about going any place else. There was an aura of magic around Walla Walla and by extension, Whitman College. But I think I would have been unhappy no matter where I had gone to school, given the luggage I was bringing with me. Whitman, at least, had the advantage of being a jewel of a campus in the loveliest setting imaginable. Surrounded by tawny wheat fields with their majestic quiet, Walla Walla was an oasis of green. It's an old town with wide, shaded streets and huge Victorian homes, one of which was built by my great-grandfather, James Knott.

I was frightened of being away from home because I thought my home—such as it was—would disintegrate if I wasn't there to keep an eye on things. Then I would lose any chance of finally getting what I wanted from my parents: enough security and love to make a home for myself in the world. My brother had moved to California saying there was nothing for him in Olympia, and that apparently included me. Though we chose opposite strategies for our survival, neither of us was equipped to get very far.

I put on a brave face and hid my confusion about life both from myself and from everyone else. Unfortunately I fooled too many adults who might have been of some help. But there was one adult who played a bit part with long-reaching effects.

I joined a Student Life Group—Cell groups, we called them—that met at the home of my first year French professor, right across the street from my Aunt Ann's old house where I had visited as a child. The Cell groups were limited to about eight students and they took on whatever flavor the professor gave them. Dr. Kopf's flavor was Feelings. He had an understanding of psychoanalysis, how much I don't know, nor did I understand what that meant. I do remember him saying many times, like a mantra, "Feelings. That's where it's at."

It sounds corny now, but in the early 70s people didn't talk all that much about feelings, although they did say "where it's at" a lot. In the Richmond family, we didn't even *have* feelings other than rage in the form of recriminations, manipulations, and martyrdom. My own rage lay dormant under the floorboards of my consciousness, expressing itself in deep scathing judgments of me but turning a smooth, pleasant face to the world. Probably the worst anyone could say about me was that I was a little goody-goody with a tendency to be clingy. My brother called me "a pious little shit."

The Cell group had found a certain amount of cohesiveness by the first semester of my sophomore year. The conversation was undirected, except that Dr. Kopf would lead us to examine the underlying feelings of anything we talked about, just like in an analytic session.

One autumn afternoon, I got a phone call from my mother. She was hysterical. She screamed that Chuck was drinking and had thrown $800 in the fire and I had to come home. Panic washed through me: something was expected of me that was beyond me. I pushed back against it and tried to get the story from my mother: He had been drinking. He had gone to Longacres racetrack and won $800 betting on the horses. He came home, drunk and happy. My mother blew up. He threw the money on the fire in the fireplace. It was hard to tell if she was more upset about his being drunk, his having been at the racetrack or the waste of $800. The phone call ended with no recognition of its effect on me.

The Cell group met that night. Contrary to what I usually did and would continue to do for years, I did not try to fake it. I took a deep breath. It all came out. Dr. Kopf was in his element because I am sure this is what he hoped to do in the Cell group: help someone. It was the first time in my life I felt listened to.

When I arrived home for Christmas break, my mother was anxious to file her report first.

"He's gone, Elena." She said dramatically. "He filed for divorce. I only wanted the separation to make him quit drinking. I don't want a divorce. He was supposed to quit drinking."

"He was supposed to quit drinking." This was her mantra for the next ten years.

It was maybe to his credit that my father didn't trash my mother through the whole ugly divorce process, but it might have been that he was just too drunk. He had retired by then so he could devote his entire day to his vodka bottle. My mother, on the other hand, was relentless in her condemnation of him, her exoneration of herself, and her pleas for me either to intercede or to not see him at all.

Alex in California said, "I don't see anything wrong with him drinking as long as he doesn't hurt himself physically."

This was a huge blow. I longed to have a big brother who loved me, and who was protective of me, and in whom I could confide, but after he didn't convince my parents to take me back to the hospital after my birth, Alex hadn't wanted much to do with me. Aside from the times we rammed our feet into each other's crotches and the one evening we listened to Bob Dylan—while remaining fully clothed—I didn't have good experiences with my brother. If I thought the divorce would draw us together, it was as much a fantasy as my mother thinking separation papers would make my father stop drinking.

I was 19 years old chronologically, but emotionally I was still 7, the age I was when my father sat on my bed and cried about how much he was suffering in his marriage. The depression I had first diagnosed in myself after reading my mother's *Good Housekeeping* was no longer festering silently in the cellar of my soul. It was beginning to burst up through the floorboards into the main rooms of the house.

Born Again Again

WHEN I RETURNED TO SCHOOL AFTER THE CHRISTMAS BREAK, I had a classic grief reaction: I fell in love. David was a skinny blond kid who played the oboe. He was in the Cell group but hadn't made much of an impression on me until the initial shock of my family's disintegration started to wane. One evening when grief was roving for some relief, I looked at him and I felt attracted. It happened in a second, like a grab for a dish falling off the counter before it smashed to pieces. I pursued him; we got acquainted and got a nice little rapport going. But I wanted love and well, not sex because I was too inhibited to even think the word, but maybe a long hug, maybe a gentle kiss.

David was a "born-again" and a part of College Life Christian Fellowship, sponsored by Inter-Varsity, an organization that evangelized college campuses. College Life met on Thursday nights for two hours of singing with guitars and discussions led by the male students. Every month a woman named Piper showed up for a few days and met with The Leadership. A very big concept, leadership; it meant Male Leadership. Even though Piper was a woman, she was ten years older than us so she had a kind of authority over the males in the same way the Virgin Mary had a kind of authority over the Son of God before he grew up.

Students made appointments to talk with her about their spiritual life and then raved about what a help she was to them. When I met with Piper to talk about the crisis in my life, we mostly talked about her worries about her future and whether or not she would get married and how she wasn't sure she wanted kids. In that it was mostly about her when it was supposed to have been mostly about me, it was kind of like talking to my mother, only without the yelling.

I visited College Life because I was trying to find a way to attract David. I liked the music: folksy songs with catchy tunes and words less graphic than:

> "On a hill far away stood an old rugged cross, the emblem of suffering and shame;"

or

> "There is a fountain filled with blood drawn from Emmanuel's vein, and sinners washed beneath that flood lose all their guilty stain."

People were friendly, and I needed friends. I didn't mind the Christian talk; some of it was downright refreshing compared to what I had grown up with and the rest I could tune out. There's no doubt that longings of every imaginable kind were ready to explode in me: a longing for a mother, a father, a brother, a friend, someone to listen to me, someone to love me; sexual and spiritual longings; longings for self-expression; and a longing to be touched that was so intense it made my back ache.

It all coalesced one night when I had my final conversion experience. I was curled up in a beanbag chair in my apartment, reading *Your God is Too Small* by JB Phillips. I made some species of request of God, after which I felt a peace wash over me and saw a light such as my mother reported my father to have seen which made him quit drinking. I was—yet again—born again.

It was like pledging a sorority! Or, more accurately, like volunteering to work in a fraternity house. In any case, I got a whole bunch of friends out of it and a group to belong to. There was a secret language that fostered a sense of acceptance. A lingo. Like the word *Fellowship.* Christians use that word a lot. You can't have coffee and cookies and chat. You are fellowshipping. *Quiet Time. Lifting our brother up in prayer.* It was important to use the right language. It was code so other Christians would know you loved the Lord and believed exactly the same things they did.

At age 19, I didn't understand that all groups have their lingo, their language. You speak it when it resonates with something inside you, but there's no monopoly on what it means. It can mean anything at all. I spoke the language because when I did, I was treated like I belonged. But as far as reaching any deep places in my heart, it didn't.

I thought I would feel loved and accepted if I was a good Christian. I had a rep for being easy to talk to. Everyone told me their life stories and their troubles. After 18 years of living with disturbed parents and two years in Dr. Kopf's Cell group, I was good at sussing out underlying feelings. People felt listened to and cared about and came back for more. This was my Christ-like version of myself. It gave me a tentative sense of belonging. And no one came at me with a fireplace poker. Admittedly my threshold for feeling accepted wasn't particularly high.

When *I* didn't feel listened to or cared about, I became outgoing and outspoken in ways that called attention to me. The shame attendant upon this kind of exposure caused dark clouds to rain just on me. At those times, I couldn't hide my depression and was consumed by a black mood. It was a relief to get away from people, crawl back inside my mind and slam the door on outside influences.

Ironically, pulling into myself looked like what a good Christian did because it took the outward form of a Quiet Time, also referred to as Going Before the Lord or Spending Time in the Word. I got up at five in the morning and spent three hours a day reading the Bible and working with books and study guides that were more sophisticated than some of the repressive, badly written things I had encountered in Sunday school. I meditated. I wrote copiously in my journals which were masterpieces of self-flagellation. I was an introspective, reflective person with a private life that I guarded assiduously. This early morning time remained my sacrament for the rest of my life, but in the beginning I spent it searching for something that I was never to find in Christianity.

The Christians at Whitman were a bunch of earnest adolescents who expected a lot from each other. We confronted each other and "held each other accountable" as we all tried to imitate Christ.

One new friend cornered me. "Elena, I feel led by the Holy Spirit to tell you that you need to start dealing seriously with God about your moods."

Years later when I asked my therapist if he would "hold me accountable" for something I was planning to do that week—probably eat less sugar— he laughed and said, "No, I'm not in the business of fomenting guilt."

A lot of my moods were in relation to David. I knew that he liked me because on the days we got together, he wrote my name in big letters on his calendar. But I felt a longing, something I hadn't felt with Richard. David was someone I wanted.

I was being coached by an upper classmate who had spent her junior year in France and was set to marry a man who had left the priesthood for her. Christine thought everyone in the world was in love. She told me that men didn't know what they felt and it required a woman to tell them. She was sure David just needed a little help.

I walked across campus to David's dorm with Christine's advice accompanying me like in a cartoon balloon. I scraped together every bit of hope and optimism I could find in my being—and it wasn't much—and enveloped it with my chaste fantasies and my inexperience.

"I'm in love with you," I said.

David received this information silently, formally, ceremoniously as a tomb, as Emily Dickinson might say. The blood drained out of his face.

"What do you, um…?" He swallowed.

"Well, um, would you hold me?"

He swallowed again. "Ok," he said.

I waited.

"Well, get over here," he said.

I didn't think it was going all that well, but I went over to where he sat and he held me briefly. That was as far as we ever got physically. Christine, my mother, and every woman I knew had told me that "men only want one thing." I wasn't entirely clear what that meant but I assumed it involved more enthusiasm than I was getting from David.

My only reference point was that this was further evidence of something wrong with me. This was confirmed when I got a visit from part of the (male) leadership of College Life who told me, "you should never tell a man that." I was devastated. Here was one of the Olympian leadership practically pronouncing me unclean. It wasn't clear whether a woman should never tell a man she loved him or just that *I* should never tell a man that I loved him because I was such a repulsive individual.

I had always felt defective. The Christianity I grew up with fostered this assessment. It was called original sin. I was born defective and needed Jesus to save me. Okay, so he had saved me a dozen times already. I wanted to feel better and to feel loved. Why wasn't that happening?

"Elena, Elena, Elena," intoned Zeus, "Feeling loved lays on the other side of a proper relationship with God."

This sounded like my mother's notions about being Right With God. It didn't explain all the perfectly happy pagans out there. Nor did it explain the Christians who went to church because it was part of the culture, but who wouldn't have dreamed of proselytizing, let alone inquiring into your soul or suggesting you be washed in blood. Now that was repulsive.

In College Life, we were brothers and sisters. No sexuality allowed, at least not as far as I could tell. God had brought together a few couples, tagged them, as it were, for eventual marriage. There were sometimes rumors that these golden couples were "struggling" but I wasn't sure what that meant. For prayer requests, guys would "offer up" their sexual fantasies, which they knew were wrong but that wouldn't go away.

Girls didn't have sexual fantasies. I certainly didn't. I had longings I couldn't express and that had no outlet. My father had used me as a buffer between him and my mother. He had dangled the possibility of a sexual relationship not by physically touching me, but by intruding to such an extent that it was not safe to fantasize about men. My mother had warned me to never call a boy, never show my intelligence. My parents' marriage consisted of one trying to make the other do something they didn't want to do. My brother had ignored me. When I left home, these were the psychic objects that accompanied me.

David was scheduled to play the oboe in a music festival in Spokane that spring. I desperately wanted to go with him.

"I could be supportive," I said. This was the approved lingo.

He looked uncomfortable. "Let me think about it," he said

My confidant, Christine, fingered her engagement ring, and said, "What does he mean by 'think?' Is he scheduling time to just sit and think? You should ask him what that means, Elena." She consulted her own experiences. "I think he's falling."

But Zeus paid me another visit on David's behalf. "David thinks you could be just as supportive if you stayed in Walla Walla," He smirked down his long Olympian nose. "Neither one of you knows what you're doing. You need to spend time in the Word to find out what God is asking of you."

Human relationships did not consist of two people facing each other, reflecting each other, and thereby getting to know each other. Instead you sat side by side, studying the Bible to find out who you were supposed to be and what you were supposed to do. Because God was Absolute Truth, there was an assumption that everyone would eventually come to more or less to the same conclusions and that would be the will of God. You would find joy in doing God's will whether you liked it or not. In practical terms, the will of God was to be found in Downer's Grove, Illinois because this is where Intervarsity Press was located and they published the study guides we used.

I grew anxious during manipulative Bible studies that tried to control thought processes and conclusions. What little appeal the Bible ever had for me came from its poetry.

("Poetry!!!" my mother shrieked. "You think that's all it is? *Poetry*?!!")

I liked Psalm 139: "You knit me together in my mother's womb, I will thank you because I am marvelously made." So far, so good. This jibed with the last time I had been happy: in the womb.

But stray lines from sermons slammed doors inside me:

"Jesus Christ has gripped us and called us to serve him."

I didn't want to be gripped, didn't want a choke hold cutting off my air. I didn't want to serve anyone. I had spent 19 years serving an emotionally disturbed mother and an alcoholic father. I wanted to feel loved. Why couldn't I be marvelously made to become who I was in a way that meant something to me and that brought love into my life? Why did it have to line up with Intervarsity Press or what the 20 year old (male) leaders on campus thought?

"He's a giant of a God you serve so make your lives count for Him."

Slam. If he was such a great God, why did he need someone like me running around making him count? In fact, this God had the same delicate ego I had been told all men have. More to the point, that my parents had.

But I hung onto Christianity because it fit a familiar pattern: if I was just good enough, I would feel the equivalent of the mother I had always needed. I would feel loved.

I thought my mother would be thrilled at my conversion, but she wasn't. She was suspicious. "Is it *Bible*- based?" I don't think my mother wanted me to be a Christian. Nor did she want my father to stop drinking. She needed some big things to complain about. She was very unhappy, and she needed some big reasons for her unhappiness.

Frances to the Rescue

I SPENT THE NEXT SUMMER WITH DON AND FRANCES. I had visited them every summer since the year I turned thirteen. Don had retired from air traffic controlling and the two of them had moved to a mobile home community in Buncombe Creek, Oklahoma, on the edge of Lake Texoma. My head still full of hope thanks to Christine, who had bagged the priest, I thought David's feelings for me would translate into something that made him want to touch me, date me. I hoped he would miss me and write to me.

At Buncombe Creek, I didn't want to pine. I wanted something to occupy me. I wanted to work in the little cafe presided over by Blanche, who sat at the counter day after day, smoking cigarettes, drinking iced tea, and staring with palpable boredom at nothing at all, thinking about the high life she had left behind in Duncan, Oklahoma.

The cafe was her husband's dream, not hers. Joe spent his days with his shirt hanging out over his dungarees, happily frying catfish and hush puppies in the kitchen. Blanche perched on a stool, impeccably made up, her black hair piled on her head and her rhinestone studded glasses on a rope around her neck.

"Why d'yawl work anyhow, Lainie? You got your whole life to work." Her bored eyes swept the café, and she blew a stream of cigarette smoke into what was a glorified bait shop with a juke box. "It ain't that great."

She looked at me. "Tell me about this boyfriend."

I dropped the bowl of soup I was transferring to the kitchen. We mopped it up together. I watched her cigarette ash fall into a puddle of soup, watched the rag come along and wipe it up.

"He's not really a boyfriend." I said. "I just want him to be. What did Frances tell you?"

"She said there was a boy you liked. Is he writin' to you?"

"No," I said sadly. "I don't really expect him to."

"Well, then he's not worth it." Her eyes flicked towards the kitchen. "And he's a fool."

My job as a waitress lasted one week. Frances and Blanche had other ideas about how I would spend the summer. Frances wanted me to enjoy myself. Blanche told me they didn't need the help.

Blanche's grandson, Todd, was a bit younger than me with the same easygoing southern ways as Frances' family. I was fascinated that kids were allowed to swear and say, "I didn't know whether to shit or go blind," but if they neglected to say "Yes ma'am" and "No sir," *that* was impolite.

Todd and I and some of the summer kids spent every afternoon on the beach of Lake Texoma. We swam, talked, told dirty jokes, and had picnics. Once they buried me in the sand and took pictures of my head sticking up out of the ground. After the tenseness of the last year, it was like taking off tight clothes and running around naked in the open air.

"Lainie, you know why the man should always be on the top? Then he'll never fuck up!"

This joke didn't alarm me when it came out of Todd's mouth. Both of us only had a vague idea of what it meant. It was innocent and adolescent.

No matter where I am in the world, and no matter the climate, I always go for walks. The first time I went for a walk at Buncombe Creek, Frances followed me out the door, "Now, Lainie, don't yawl go far. Yawl aren't used to this heat, baby doll. Don't you want to take the truck?"

"What, for a walk?" I waved at her and headed for the lake.

It wasn't any cooler near the water but I waded for a bit, and then started back. Five minutes out, I started to feel a little faint, then a little nauseated. As if on cue, a cloud of dust signaled Frances' arrival in the blue pickup truck.

"I knew you were goin' for a walk, no matter what, but yawl aren't used to this heat!" she said cheerfully.

I crawled gratefully into the truck. Frances never understood the charms of a walk but she rarely tried to prevent me from taking one. I think Frances might say that she understood the charms of the Richmonds and they were all stubborn as hell.

While coming back along the same dirt road later that week, a car pulled up alongside me and a voice drawled, "Yawl wanna ride?" I climbed in next to three children and we chatted all the way back to Don and Frances' bungalow.

"I couldn't figure out *what* she was doin' or if she was out there for *exercise* or what!" The woman told Frances.

"This is my niece, Lainie. She's from Seattle," Frances said as though this explained everything. Just in case it didn't, she added, "She's not used to this heat."

Frances and I went on a diet that summer. I had never followed an honest to God diet before. Frances bought the eggs, canned spinach, and grapefruit. We quit a few days shy of the second week because we were so crabby we couldn't stand each other. Frances lost 15 pounds and I gained 4.

There was a long-playing record of Marian Anderson in the house and I played it until I learned every song. I had my guitar with me and I figured out chords for "My Lord What a Morning," "Swing Low Sweet Chariot," and a few others and sang them for anyone who wanted to listen. I had a little program I called *Medley for Buncombe Creek* that I sang for Don and Frances one night. Soon they had me singing for everyone in the community. My show opened with "Nelly Bly" and "Beautiful Brown Eyes," moved through the "Blue Tail Fly," "Old Smoky," "The Crawdad Song," "Mockingbird Hill" and half a dozen others until it ended with "Red River Valley." Everyone knew all the songs. They were the songs I wanted to hear on the cafe jukebox but everything coming out of that was Nashville.

Midway through the summer, Richard called from Kentucky. He'd gotten the phone number from my mother in Olympia. On his way to the west coast, he wanted to come see me. He and I had corresponded since my summer in Kentucky because he kept writing me letters and I didn't know that I didn't have to respond. In the world of my upbringing, nobody cared what a woman wanted. Everyone assumed that women all wanted the same thing: male attention, marriage, and children. You weren't supposed to be picky about men. If a man was interested, you counted yourself lucky. If you weren't interested in the man, you were just a little scared and that was normal, but it wasn't advisable to let him Slip Through Your Fingers.

I was not just a little scared, I was aghast. Because everyone seemed so excited, I did not convey to Frances how much I wanted the whole thing to go away. I remembered Richard as someone who talked about himself and assigned his own meaning to my responses. He interacted with the woman he imagined I was and I didn't know how to assert myself. For his purposes, I didn't need to be there at all. I felt like I was hanging off the end of one of my mother's non-sequiturs.

Richard's pursuit terrified me. What the hell did he want? Was this romance? Wasn't romance supposed to feel good? This felt like my father leering at me in a darkened theater.

If I had expressed this, Frances would have put the kibosh on the visit—"Ain't nobody goin' to do Lainie that way." But all she knew was that I was inexperienced and frightened. She thought it would be good for me to have a gentleman caller. But she did reassure me that she and Don would be around all weekend.

My mind whited out for much of the time Richard was there. We waltzed to something coming in on the radio and it felt to me as though my father had leapt up on the stage where I was dancing in the school play. Midway through the dance, Richard went to the bathroom and came back smelling of mouthwash. This frightened me. Why was he thinking about his breath around me? I just wanted him to go away.

We sat out under the trees his last evening and he took my hand and started saying things to me that made me want to faint with anxiety. Things about my hair and how sweet my face was. I was stunned. I didn't know how to flirt. I didn't know I could take my hand away if I didn't want to be touched. I chattered about dump trucks and robins, anything other than my lovely hair and my fine skin until finally it seemed reasonable to say I was tired and wanted to go to bed.

"Oh Lainie," Frances said to me later. "If I had known you were having to chatter, I would have rescued you." I was mystified that Frances understood so much just from the report that I had been chattering. If we had talked about it further, Frances might have explained to me that romance only feels good if both people want it. My idea of closeness involved one person making another person do something they didn't want to do. I didn't want to be the one on the bottom. I didn't want to be "done to." That was how being with Richard felt. With David I had experienced the frustration of trying to be the one who "does to." That felt just as bad.

The summer deteriorated. Don was an alcoholic just like my father. When he was working, he kept the drinking under reasonable control because he was good at a job where it was important to be alert. But after he retired, he spent most of his days a big sodden mess. He was an even uglier drunk than my father. Frances drank with him because she wasn't about to be left out. I watched them get drunk the way I had watched my father. When they got to a certain level, if they were still in the house, I went someplace else. All the residents knew me so there was always a place to go. But more often than not, Don and Frances were off partying and I was alone in the house.

I was alone in the house the night a tornado swept through the southern part of the state. I lay in bed listening to the wind and wondering if there would be a good lightning storm to watch. I was the only person in the community that wasn't in a storm shelter. I didn't know where the shelters were or how to know when it was time to be in one. We didn't have tornados in the Pacific Northwest. As it happened, the tornado spared Buncombe Creek.

Don and Frances came home around 4:00 that morning and slept late. By noon they were sitting in their Barcaloungers, looking stunned.

"What time d'you get in, baby doll?"

"I was here all night," I said.

"Why, you little fool! You could have died last night if that thing had come through here. Lainie. You don't have the sense God gave a goat!"

I looked at them. They would probably stay drunk for another five days. I decided I would go home 3 weeks earlier than planned.

I came home on the train. I boarded Amtrak at Ardmore, Oklahoma and rode to Chicago where I got on the Empire Builder to come across the country to Seattle.

The rest of my years at Whitman were lacerated by my parents' divorce and the unhappy relationship with David. At Whitman David alternated between ignoring me and trying to be friendly, creating a limbo neither of us had the life skills to resolve. On breaks I went home to my divorced and warring parents who had carved out their own private level of hell.

They fought constantly. They fought over who would pay my tuition, my mother occasionally refusing to contribute and thus using my college future as a way to score over my father. That winter semester my father was so drunk, he was unable to hold the pen to sign the tuition check that was already overdo. I needed to have it with me when I went back after Christmas.

I had to make a visit to the dean of students, a man not known for his warmth. I stammered that my father was drunk and couldn't sign the check but he would be able to eventually and I would get the tuition paid as soon as possible. I was flushed, near tears and oh, so humiliated. The dean looked at me with distaste. His thick lips and fish eyes bulged further, filling up with his own disgust. I stared back at him, horrified.

"Get it to us as soon as you can," he said. He rustled some papers. We were done.

I bumbled along. I joined Alpha Phi sorority in my junior year and went to some fraternity functions, got into sophomoric mischief, and had some good times. I was my sorority's song leader and I rehearsed our group for the annual choral contest, an old and venerable tradition at Whitman. We sang Pablo Casal's "Nigra Sum," and a funny little round called "So She Went into the Garden." We won.

My friend, Scott, was the first to find me and give me a big hug.

"I didn't pay all that much attention to the music, Elena. I was watching your butt move!" he said impishly

I flushed with pleasure. I didn't feel uncomfortable hearing such a reference to my body. It was a lovely experience for me.

Scott was in my class but a year older. He had already spent a year in the Navy reserves and still went off once a month to drill. So he was more of a grownup than those of us who had arrived at Whitman fresh out of high school and had parents paying our tuition. He was a part of College Life but didn't seem to buy into the Christian jargon du jour. He told me once that he didn't need the resurrection of Christ to be a Christian. He had his own ideas. He was a psychology major. That will do it.

Around the World

THE YEAR AFTER I GRADUATED FROM WHITMAN, I embarked on a 10 week trip with a Christian group that called itself *The Yielded*. My association with *The Yielded* was a tour of duty to buff my Christian credentials. We went around the world beginning in Los Angeles, California at the home of the leaders, a couple in their 40s. Rick and Phyllis had set up a ministry whereby they accosted and tried to convert people who came to play on the ocean beaches of southern California. They modeled themselves after Francis and Edith Schaeffer, on whom they had a huge crush. Frances Schaeffer was a Protestant theologian who had a degree of influence over American evangelical Christianity in the 70s and 80s.

Thanks to Schaeffer, Humanism became a big, bad word in Christian circles. It even reached my mother's down-market church's teaching. She followed me around the house one day lecturing me about my attitude (bad), my opinions (wrong), and my future if I continued down the path I was on (Hell).

Finally she gathered her energies and red in the face, hissed at me, "It's Humanism! Humanism!" She paused to let the word sink in. "Do you know what that means? Elena?"

"Yes," I said. "I do. I studied it for four years at Whitman College. You paid for it."

Another piece of semantics we tripped over was the word *relationship*. I came home from college my head full of ideas about Community and Being in a Relationship. But the first time I used the R word, she looked suspicious and disgusted,

"Just exactly what do you mean by Relationship?" she asked.

This took me by surprise until I recognized her Sex is Disgusting tone of voice; I remembered that in the 50s, when people were having illicit or adulterous sex, they were said to be having A Relationship.

"Friends, Mom," I said. "I mean friends."

There were 40 of us on the trip; most of the kids were a few years younger than I and they all were in thrall to Rick and Phyllis. I wasn't. Part of the trip required us to listen to Frances Schaeffer writings as regurgitated by Rick and to put up with Phyllis throwing temper tantrums when things didn't go her way. She told us on the first day that she looked at all of us as a doctor might look at patients; she wanted to heal us, although the revolting expression she used was "to fix us." I privately thought that I would have changed doctors.

At LAX, the day we left, I asked Rick what he was looking forward to most on the trip, since he obviously enjoyed traveling. This was an attempt, on my part, to assess the amount of sucking up I might have to do in order to protect myself.

"I'm not looking forward to traveling," he said. "I'm here to be involved in people's lives."

That had a bad smell to it. But in spite of the leaders, it was a remarkable experience for me.

It was 1977, and we spent 10 weeks traveling around the world, visiting 20 countries at the cost of $3000. Because we were Christians out to reach the world for Christ, we saw things I would never have seen on a conventional trip. We visited a leprosarium in Korea. At the gloriously smelly fish market in Pusan, my travel nausea left and didn't return until I threw up outside the Manger of the Christ Child in Bethlehem. I contributed my watch to the bribe we assembled to get us off the plane in the Rangoon airport. I sat and talked with a man being fed in a soup kitchen in Calcutta. We visited a Tibetan Refugee Center in Kathmandu. I changed money on the black market in Lahore and haggled for pen knives on Chicken Street in Kabul. We went into Bulgaria where all the peasant women looked like my grandmother with their long skirts and head scarves.

In the 21st century, people are usually impressed to hear I have been in Afghanistan but my entrance into that country was not particularly impressive. I had been suffering for days from constipation. I was frankly happy to avoid toilets in India and Pakistan but after a week I was very uncomfortable. So I consumed an entire bag of dried prunes. Then I got on the bus that would take us through the Khyber Pass to Kabul. The buses were rattletrap, as loose as I was bound up, bumping along the ancient road with its ruts and rocks, curves and twists. Long before we arrived, I was in absolute agony. The end results were explosive and prolonged.

Every few nights we had to assemble for some sort of Christian teaching. The Schaeffer theology attempted to bring a Christian perspective to art. I didn't agree with his opinions, but I recognized that he was a thinker, trying to bring a contemporary perspective to ancient beliefs. But as regurgitated by Rick, it was thoroughly boring. There was a darker aspect as well: we were fed arrogance with our scripture, as if, as Americans, we needed any more of that. Rick conveyed no sense that we had anything to learn from other cultures. But I was clear in my own mind that I was along to see the world, not to convert it.

The 14th century Kinkaku-ji Temple in Kyoto sits in the water of a large lake, surrounded by damp, thick forests. As we rounded a corner of the woods and came into the clearing, the temple loomed in a silence that felt alive. I could have stood there forever.

I was joined by one young woman in the group who said, "Isn't this sad?" We had been encouraged to pity the Buddhists, who were so impoverished, they didn't even have a god.

"I find it peaceful," I said.

In Switzerland we visited L'Abri, home of the idols, the Schaeffer's. The royal couple was not in residence but we were treated to an afternoon with one of their associates who explained why Beethoven's four last quartets were Satanic. It had something to do with the amount of dissonance.

I tried to keep my opinions to myself, but I was a grandiose 22 years old. In one of Rick's lectures where instead of being out in the exotic locale, we were stuck in a conference room in an American style hotel, I asked why he only talked about painting, sculpture, or music; why not literature, especially poetry?

"Poetry leaves me cold."

"So because poetry leaves you cold, it isn't an art form? What about Shakespeare? His plays are so rich."

"Shakespeare is humanistic. He glorifies humanity, not the Lord."

I started to argue but he cut me off, "This is not a discussion group. I am teaching."

His groupies rallied around him, "Can we just go on?" they whined.

Rick glared at me and I stopped paying attention.

The trip ticked on. Rick told me that I did not respect (male) authority. I thought, "What, you mean yours?"

My contact lenses began bothering me early in the trip. In the Middle East I asked Rick if there was a way I could see an eye doctor.

"When we get to Israel," he said "I'll take care of it."

Then it was "When we get to Greece…when we get to Italy."

Finally in Italy I overheard him asking our tour guide about a hair appointment for Phyllis. I elbowed my way to our guide and told her I needed to see an eye doctor. Within the hour, the guide took me personally to an Italian optometrist who cleaned the grunge off my contacts, checked my eyes and didn't charge me.

I sought Rick out at dinner. "You know, I waited for you to help me with the contact lens thing because you said you would. But your wife's hair appointment was more important." My voice was shaking but I swallowed and charged ahead. "If I don't respect authority, this might be a reason why."

Rick looked at me with no discernable expression. "I don't have any patience with contact lenses. They're a fad. You have your glasses with you."

When I didn't leave—I was waiting for an apology—he frowned. If this was going to be a "conversation" he had further complaints to unload. "I don't have any patience with you women and your menstrual cramps, either. It's all in your head."

I looked across the table at Phyllis's head. At least she had gotten her hair done.

I did the entire 10 weeks with three changes of clothes in a half empty suitcase. The guys carried the big pieces of luggage and they all wanted to carry my suitcase but that was the extent to which I felt wanted. In the first four weeks of the trip, I had very few friends. Almost no one chose to sit with me on the buses and trains. As people filed on, I would look out the window so I wouldn't have to watch all the rejection. I had never been a team player. If we had been an Agatha Christie story, I would have been the one everyone wanted to murder. I can see that now, but at the time I just felt out of place and unhappy.

My only real friend on that trip was a young man named John. We were immediately drawn to one another and as we came around the world, we spent more and more time together, talking and laughing. John had a smile so big it made the rest of his face disappear. One night he told me he was dying. He had terminal leukemia and this was his last big fling. He said he was careful about who he told because people "got weird." In the 70s, in Christian circles, cancer, divorce, and alcoholism were all lumped together with the same stigma. I was acquainted with two out of those three, so I knew something about how people "got." It seemed the most natural thing in the world for John to have chosen to tell me. For much of the trip, I was the only person who knew.

I started to enjoy myself in the last few weeks, thanks to John and a few other kids who warmed to me after a fashion. I had a fabulous time in England and Scotland. We stayed in a castle in Crieff, saw two (humanistic) Shakespeare plays in Stratford, and had four lecture-free days running around London on our own. We saw the Dickens house and the Sam:Johnson house and had tea in a Lyons Corner House. We went to services at St Paul's Cathedral and toured the Poet's Corner at Westminster Abbey, where I did not run into Rick. I recited Wordsworth's sonnet on Westminster Bridge. I bought a pair of colorful suspenders for John in a shop near 221 Baker Street because I couldn't find a deerstalker hat for him.

John came up to Seattle in the spring of the following year. He wanted to talk about us getting married. Oddly enough, it wasn't his illness that put me off; it was the sheer terror of a man wanting to be close.

We went for a walk in the neighborhood. I picked little blossoms off the overhanging trees as we made small talk. There was a long pause.

He burst out, "I like you so much. Everything you do is lovely. Even the way you are picking those flowers."

I liked John. I might have fallen in love with him. He was kind and he made me laugh. I wasn't afraid to marry someone who was probably going to die soon.

But I couldn't take in his love. I could only let my sexual and romantic feelings flower around someone who, like David, showed little interest in me. When I was sure there was no possibility of reciprocity, I had room to feel my own feelings. But when I felt a man's desire, I froze. My breasts made my father anxious. The possibility that he might come in and look at me sleeping naked was presented as a concrete thing to be afraid of. I had no room to imagine anything playful, let alone exciting. Sex was a deadly serious game.

John was hurt and disappointed. He went back to California; we wrote a few times. He died the next year.

No Sex Please, We're Religious

AFTER THE TRIP AROUND THE WORLD, I found a job teaching music, first in Head Start, then in a private school called Perkins Musical Kindergarten. I liked kids. I played guitar and knew hundreds of songs. Even though I wasn't singing the classical music that I loved, I was willing to sing anything with great words, a good tune and interesting rhythms.

I moved to the University district and into a house stocked with other Whitman alumni. I acquired a boyfriend as conflicted about closeness as I was. Andy was short and stocky and made me laugh with his quick wit and sarcasm.

He lettered a large sign: YOU DRIVE LIKE A JERK that he calmly put in the window of his car when someone annoyed him in traffic. Sometimes he wore a gorilla mask when he drove around town. This was the 1970s before road rage and outrageous talk shows. No one else I knew did things like that. I loved sitting in the front seat when Andy was up to his antics. Andy loved my sense of humor.

He was a different breed altogether from David at Whitman, who showed little interest in me, or Richard from Kentucky, who showed too much. We liked each other but with a roughly equal degree of reservations about sex. We were copacetic because we both were funny and we both had emotional difficulties, although in our relationship, it was his difficulties that were front and center, not mine. I was supposed to be supportive. That suited me. My ability to hide myself was so well honed that even I couldn't find me.

Hiding myself certainly suited the Christian community I was involved in. I had discussions with other women about the two tasks young men were said to have as they matured: find their career path and find their partner. It never occurred to me or, apparently, to anyone I talked to, including married women with daughters of their own, that a young woman might have those same tasks; that they didn't arrive at age 21, fully matured and ready to do nothing more than a man's laundry. The women's liberation movement was addressing these imbalances, but the movement swirled around our doors and didn't so much as leak through a crack until long after I had lost interest in trying to be a Christian.

Physical contact was not encouraged unless the couple was engaged but that was hardly Andy's and my problem. Both of us were hesitant to do more than hold hands. Andy's uncertainty made it safe to feel my desire; but following a map in my mind that had been drawn long ago, I found my desire sitting next to "Here Be Dragons." In maneuvering around the dragons, imagining that I was unattractive was preferable to feeling that my desire left me at the mercy of whatever a man might want from me.

It was dangerous to want a man because he might do icky things like invade my bedroom with his drunkenness. When my father sat on my bed and complained about his marriage, he invaded psychic space that should have been reserved for my innocence. He made it dangerous to feel close to him. There were frightening consequences to being daddy's little girl and I hadn't matured past that. I felt desire for men but that desire became an infection trapped in scar tissue, and with no outlet.

I talked to the pastor of the church we attended. I was confused about myself and the relationship with Andy. The pastor told me that since I loved Andy, I could—with God's grace—set my own needs aside. Not even with God's grace. Women made those sorts of sacrifices, it was their nature. As much as this hurt, it was familiar. It didn't occur to me that I could look in other places for more satisfying choices. Or for a choice at all.

It never occurred to me that what other people said came out of their own subjectivity. When it came to intimate relationships, I saw everyone as being an expert and myself as a small child who didn't know anything. I sussed out the safety of other people while attempting to get whatever felt like love just as I had done with an alcoholic father and an emotionally disturbed mother.

The Christian Charismatic movement was blowing through the land and Andy and I were caught up in a power that effectively displaced sex and intimacy. At our church, Good Samaritan Episcopal, folks were actually raising their hands when they sang. Episcopalians. If you wanted to speak in tongues, there were places to go where you could receive the laying on of hands, fall down, and come up off the floor, babbling away. It was called being "slain in the spirit" and it wasn't just for speaking in tongues. You could go and have it done to you just like a hair appointment, every week. The Lord wanted to BLESS YOU, praise God!

We were Whitman graduates, listening to tapes and reading the books of Malcolm Smith, Kenneth Copeland, Kenneth Hagen, and Dennis and Rita Bennett, the Rock Stars of the movement. We commanded demons to come out of rocks. We claimed our healing in the name of the Lord, refusing to believe sickness could get a toehold, even while goo was oozing out our noses.

I fasted for 10 days. With the help of the Holy Spirit, of course. I drank water, nothing else. By the 10th day I was weak and felt like I was in a high altitude. Up there with the angels. See, that was the hand of the Lord, praise Jesus. By the end of the fast, I was speaking in tongues and that just about proved everything. It was a heady time.

Andy and I could both be street fighters when protecting our particular vulnerabilities. These tendencies looked askance at our self-righteous spirituality but we human beings are great at conjuring temporary amnesia when we need to. We were also trying to carry on a sexual relationship without the sex and without understanding why we were both so afraid. We weren't the first couple to discover that making sex wear a religious overcoat didn't put out the fire, it made the inevitable explosion all the more spectacular.

I made dinner one night for the two of us. In the 70s, in left leaning Christian circles, we were all trying to be vegetarian. I made borscht, coleslaw, and cornbread. I set the table with Rosie, my roommate's china. I ladled the soup into a tureen and set it on the table. I poured honey into a small bowl and set it next to the butter. The salad dressing was a bit runny because I had attempted to make my own mayonnaise. Andy brought a bottle of red wine, which he poured into Rosie's wine glasses.

Andy had a sheaf of papers he needed help collating. He was giving a talk about "Godly relationships" later in the evening. As I listened to him expound on his model for a Godly relationship, the reality of our relationship sank into the borscht, as it were. Andy viewed our inability to be physically involved as a virtue, and was using our relationship as some kind of model. I had temporarily forgotten that as a Christian I was expected to be free of fear. Andy was taking the position that he had never known anything except the peace of God that passes understanding. The pressure from these impossible standards was kindling to the fire of our humanity.

"This doesn't feel right at all." I said. "You and I—we're not a great model for happy. I'm not happy. I'm afraid about what isn't happening with us."

My fear was the lit match thrown into the stove; it activated Andy's fears. A wild look came into his eyes.

"You're a child of God! What the hell are you talking about fear for? Don't use that word! Words bring the fear into being!" He shouted hysterically. "You're making it *happen* right now just by saying it!"

"Making what happen? *Nothing's* happening. That's the whole point!"

"Shut UP!"

"You shut up!"

But he wouldn't shut up. His voice came at me, a tsunami of rage. It felt like my mother barging into my room with her wild prohibitions about men, sex, and menstruation. It felt like my father's anxiety about my sexuality; an anxiety so overwhelming, he had to ejaculate all over me by making unseemly remarks about my thirteen year old breasts. That had happened at a dinner table, too.

I looked down at my hands, which were clutching the edges of the table to keep myself from being blown away. I watched them come up, slow motion, the table still in them. I watched myself tip its contents into Andy's lap. Everything slid onto him, the borscht, the red wine, the runny coleslaw dressing, the honey, the dishes and the glasses.

He leaped up. "You BITCH!" he screamed.

Two shades of red soaked into his beige jacket and shirt. I stared at the streams of mayonnaise and blobs of honey carrying cornbread crumbs and flecks of cabbage into his crotch and down his thighs. I was too stunned to laugh.

He grabbed his lecture notes about Godly relationships and ran out of the house.

After my heart stopped racing, after Rosie and I cleaned up the mess in the kitchen, after I wrote down the name of her china pattern,

I felt euphoric. It was not at all pleasing to the Lord but it was mighty satisfying to me. That was the beginning of the end of me and Andy. We broke up shortly after that. I chose the classic solution for getting over a man. I went abroad.

La Misérable

I HAD ALWAYS LOVED THE IDEA OF LIVING IN EUROPE in some charming, colorful, quaint village where people sang folk songs and bought flowers every day. This was my idea of what France would be like. There was a Christian Bible school 40 miles from Paris that ran, in large part, with the help of American volunteers. Having been on a Yielded Cruise, I was in the pipeline to work *au pair* at the Ecole. I thought I would sign on for two years and if it worked out, I'd stay for five. I lasted five months.

From the moment I got there, all I wanted to do was to come home. I had flown to London on New Year's Eve. A friend had slipped me some of her Librium and I had taken it an hour before I was to board, but takeoff was delayed for three hours. I staggered onto the plane, fell asleep and missed dinner. I had the day to kill in London, which, in January, did not offer the same welcome as during a warm week in August. I got on the evening boat-train to Paris, which was what people did before there was a Chunnel. The boat-train, the old London-Paris route, was miserably cold and lonely.

By the time I got to the Gare du Nord and had managed to get myself into a taxi to take me to St Lazare, I was so overwhelmed I could not bear to even look out the window. I stared at my hands. It had been about 32 hours since I had left Seattle. Panic welled up inside me, a species of fear that would be my familiar companion for the next 25 years, but at the time, I didn't know what it was. I only felt that if I looked up, I would disintegrate.

At the station for the Ecole, someone picked me up and took me to the facility where I would be living and working for—God help me—as short a time as I possibly could. It was a dirty, dilapidated villa in what seemed to be a giant vacant lot. There had been a storm during the night and parts of the roof had blown off and were lying around the yard. I looked at it in horror. This was home? Was I to be one of those poor females in a Gothic novel?

The au pairs' quarters were in the back of the villa, with an outside entrance. In addition, there was a passageway through the basement (le cave) that led to the kitchen, where I washed floors and potatoes, and prepared tea every afternoon for the students. My flat mates, two Americans and one French woman, kept the Ecole clean and helped with cooking and office work. The Americans worked for three months at a time, left the country briefly to renew their tourist visas, and came back. This could go on for years.

I was dreadfully homesick. That, in itself, wasn't unusual. It was a foreign country and I was far away from home. It takes months to acclimate to even the most gentle of situations. Most of the Americans I met that winter were homesick, but everyone coped in a different way. I talked. The worse I felt, the more I talked. Usually I kept things to myself but I was away from familiar social cues. My anxiety was so intense, it flipped me inside out.

For five months, I was either deeply depressed or so filled with anxiety that I couldn't think. I had spontaneous fits of sobbing. The response to this was impatience and annoyance that I was neither snapping out of it nor shutting up about it. I still thought of myself as a Christian. In the face of Christianity's practical uselessness to me, I persisted in concluding that there was something terribly wrong with me, not It.

There was an English language library at the Ecole; books smeared with the sweat and tears of homesick Americans. I read *Scenes From Clerical Life*, *Les Miserables*, *Jane Eyre*, and *A Movable Feast*. I read J.I. Packer's *Knowing God* three times, taking so many notes I practically copied the book in its entirety.

I didn't have any revelations about God. In fact, reading that book, studying the Bible and talking with other Christians was a lot like speaking the French language. It meant nothing to me. I plugged in a word or phrase and if I got a response, I knew I had communicated something. If I was still standing upright, then whatever had taken place hadn't hurt me.

I took long walks. I walked up hills into the neighboring villages or down along the Seine. I walked to the closest town, where I regularly got into violent misunderstandings with the officials at Le Poste because I always asked for the equivalent of 10 stamps equaling 2 francs, 80 centimes each.

"Pourquoi?" they demanded.

"Why?" I translated silently. "You're asking me 'Why?' Because I want them and I have the money to pay for them. What business is it of yours?"

An aerogram to America, which was the usual way to send a letter in those days, was 1 F 80. It was beyond me to explain that I was writing 5 and 6 page letters to America and that I had weighed the paper at the Ecole so I knew how much postage I needed.

I might have saved the postage because as I learned later, the recipients of my letters home were not happy with me. My father encouraged me to stick it out, saying it was bound to get easier. My mother wrote that it hadn't been *her* decision to go to France. A friend told me she was so disgusted with my complaining she had stopped opening my letters.

With few exceptions, the rest of my Christian community in Seattle was condemning, or a notch or two above judgmental. Did I not understand that this was the only Protestant school for 200 million people—all of them apparently living with the ghastly choice of either the Ecole or idolatrous Catholicism? Did I think I was going to be treated like a Queen? I needed to Go Before God, Seek the Lord, study the Bible and stop going off by myself so much. I needed to be with people to get my mind off myself.

But when I was with people, I was yelled at a lot. The cook was always on a tear about something and tended to take things out on me. The housekeeper seemed to seek me out to give her someone to scold. One of the Americans went off on me and yelled that I was selfish and self-involved. Even the French dogs—the *chiens mechants*, the "mean dogs"—barked at me when I walked through the villages. Once one of them leaped a wall and bit me in the leg.

It was reminiscent of my growing up years. The difference being that when my mother yelled at me, I yelled back and that gave me a sense of power, which was not really what I needed. I needed a Mother. I needed someone who was wholeheartedly my advocate; someone who could help me understand my own feelings. There was no one who could tell me, with any authority, that my feelings were completely normal, that traveling was disorienting and homesickness was common; that when you live in another country, the first year can be quite awful.

Except Juliet, a woman in Seattle whose acquaintance I had made a few months before leaving for France. Juliet's parents were doctor-missionaries in South America, so Juliet had grown up overseas. At a very early age, she had been shipped off to boarding schools. She knew loneliness. She knew the feeling of being a motherless child. She was also a Christian so fed up she was about to blow up. She wrote compassionate, encouraging letters and sent me care packages. A long-distance friendship bloomed.

In March, I went to Germany to get a dated passport stamp, thus making it "legal" for me to be working in France while on a tourist visa. The American owners of the school were very proud that their volunteers all had current three month tourist visas, in case anyone should come nosing around. How they would pass us off as tourists was apparently a problem they hoped never to have.

I loved Germany. In fairness, I will say that people bought flowers in both countries, but that was the extent of any realized fantasies about France. Germany was more what I had had in mind. It was colorful and tidy. It was spring, it was warm. People were friendly and open to me. In France, where I could form complete French sentences and use them in context, I got used to being snubbed and told to speak English. In Germany, I was practically mauled if I said "Bitte." One storekeeper came out from behind the counter and kissed me.

On my way back to the Ecole, the train crossed into France in the middle of the night. German officials woke up our compartment, collected our passports, disappeared into the hall, and returned the documents a few minutes later. I was on the SNCF when I saw there was no visa stamp in my passport. I noticed there wasn't a stamp from when I first entered the country in January either. There was no paper trail that I had ever been in France. There was only the intensity of my wishing I had never come at all.

Back at the Ecole, I didn't have any more sense than to say something about it. If I had kept mum, as I had in second grade during the leaking milk carton interrogation, I could have saved myself some unpleasantness. If discovered, the worst consequence for me would, I suppose, be deportation, which made me wonder about the French for "turn myself in." But of course nothing like that happened. What happened is that the owners of the Ecole yelled at me.

"You didn't *ask for the visa?*"

"I didn't know I needed to."

"They don't always stamp. *You have to ask them.*"

"I didn't know that."

Here were two people who expected me to know something and do something, primarily because they were concerned about how it made them look. Welcome home, Elena.

I found grace and small mercies in bits and pieces wherever I could. By May, I was finding my way more easily and having some good experiences. I took French classes at the Alliance Francaise in St Germain en laye. There I met Mavis, a British woman who befriended me. She thought it was a shame that whoever my people were, they had not introduced me properly to Paris. So she did. For several weekends in May, she took me around the city. We visited Au Deux Magots, Montmartre, L'eglise de St Germain, the Tuileries, the Louvres.

I loved being with a Brit. In front of a Renoir at the Jeu de Paume, Mavis said "Now wasn't it clever of the chap to put that bit of light just there?"

At the Place de la Concord, we wanted to have a look at the Obelisk, so Mavis showed me how to cross a street in Paris. She took my arm and said calmly, "Now it's best to just start out at a normal pace and keep walking at the same speed."

"WHAT?" Ten cars barreled down the boulevard toward us.

"It's all right. They'll go around us."

They didn't even slow down, they just zipped around us, as did the stream of cars behind them. It was exhilarating in a hysterical kind of way.

Back at the Gothic horror that was the Ecole, I found kindness in another American named Phillip. He worked at a construction site for new dormitories and also took French classes at the Alliance Francaise. Five mornings a week, Phillip and I and a Greek student, whom everyone referred to as "le Grec," huddled on the platform as we waited for the train to Paris. In the afternoons, I sought Phillip out at the construction site and talked with him for hours while he mixed cement or laid brick. We talked about religion, but it was his friendship, not his theology, that was a grace and a mercy for me.

Many of the French staff were sympathetic but reserved. They had seen a lot of homesick Americans come and go. Virginie was soft and sweet and would do that air-kiss thing on my cheeks before sitting down to talk with me. Marie-Therese said that I was missing "le joie." She would pray for me to have "le joie." She didn't think it was my fault that I lacked "le joie." The Africans on staff were also homesick. They spoke gently and seemed to like my expressiveness, so I got on with them.

My French roommate taught me French songs whose tunes stay with me still, even though the language no longer comes as easily as it once did. I loved the French version of the Hokey Pokey, particularly the line "je danse le Boogie Woogie" with the stress on the second syllable of Woogie. A little berceuse, "Demain matins, petit garcon," was charming. One of the Christian songs, "Je louai l'eternel," had a majestic melody. The words had no charge for me because I never succeeded in thinking in French. So "Je louai l'eternel" in my head became "I love the eternal," a comfortably pagan sentiment.

Then there was Jessica, the four-year-old daughter of a couple of American volunteers. Jessie was my *petite amie*, a blonde child with translucent skin and blue eyes that assessed the world with no sentimentality. Dressed by her mother with admonitions to not get her frilly blue dress, white tights and shiny Mary Janes dirty, she turned her angelic face to me, went cross-eyed, and whispered, "Merde!"

Jessie and I spent afternoons on the Seine collecting wine bottle corks and escargot shells. We brought them home by the handfuls and made them into mosaics and trivets. Extrapolating, Jessie rummaged through her parents' trash and sorted out things that matched. She collected empty toilet paper rolls under her bed.

"Elena can *use* them!" she said reproachfully when her mother tried to throw them out.

We sang songs, baked cookies, and went for walks together. I listened to her age four assessment of her world and it softened the edges of mine.

Cornish Bred

I LEFT FRANCE FOR GOOD ON MY BIRTHDAY, June 17, and crossed the Channel to England. It was my birthday present to myself. I spent several days in London and visited Oxford and Cambridge. A book called *In the Steps of Jane Austen* took me to Chawton, Winchester, and Bath. I spent two miserable nights in a mildewed Bed and Breakfast in Tunbridge Wells just to visit Penshurst Place because I was enamored of Sir Phillip Sidney.

I went to Cornwall. After visiting Penzance, Mousehole, and St Ives, I got on the Tamar Valley line at Plymouth. This Little Engine That Could took me to Harrowbarrow, the Cornish village where my great grandfather was born, and where my father's family—maternal side—goes back generations. My Aunt Ann had corresponded with the Cornish relations all her life and had sent care packages during the Second World War. When she died, I found Miss Hazel White in her address book. Hazel and I had been corresponding for several years when I arrived to meet her for the first time.

The Tamar Valley train was two cars long and I shared it with Cornish women and men coming home from Plymouth market. I was the last passenger at the end of the line. I was left on a platform standing in a field, surrounded by shrubs. The train belched its way back down the hill and I was left alone with my suitcase. There was no one in sight and nothing but sky and foliage in every direction. I thought, "How did I get here and why didn't anyone stop me?"

Hazel's niece and nephew, Pamela and Mervyn, came bumping along in their car before too long. They had already been to the "station" twice to see if the train had come in. Hazel, age 68, was awaiting me at home with the teapot and the clotted cream. She lived in a string of miner's cottages that had been converted into one house. I had a room with antique furniture, a sink, and a huge bed covered with a glorious apricot colored duvet. To get to the bathroom, I had to go down a flight of stairs in what had been the middle cottage, through the sitting room, into the kitchen and up the stairs of what had been the north cottage.

During my week in Harrowbarrow, every speck of family came through to meet the American cousin. They talked to me as though I was one of them and not a complete stranger. Pamela's mother said to me, "I imagine ye were tired from your journey, but that's all. It's not like ye were comin' to strangers; ye were comin' to family."

Hazel's neighbor, with whom she regularly ate an orange at 8 p.m., had told her that Americans preferred coffee to tea.

"You don't know how to make coffee. Coo, whatchoo going to do, Hazel?"

I told Hazel I preferred tea. I had preferred tea ever since I first read *Pride and Prejudice.* She clapped her hands, "Oh, lovely!" When she found I took it with milk, she said, "Coo, she's Cornish bred, she is." Thereafter she introduced me as her American cousin, adding, "she likes tea."

I was awakened every morning with a cup of tea and a rich tea biscuit. We had tea every two hours throughout the day. Tea when we returned from a walk, tea after a bath, tea after chatting over the fence with the neighbor, tea after pruning the roses, tea after looking at family pictures, tea after it had been two hours. A loaf of bread had been ordered from the Post Office store especially for my visit. The short walk up the road to collect it required a cuppa before setting out and after returning 10 minutes later.

Tea came in on the trolley, along with the digestives, rich tea biscuits, Congress tarts, currant muffins, cheese pastry, scones, or the last piece of Christmas cake with marzipan icing, frozen since December; always with clotted cream, and usually with strawberries, this being June. And that was just for the cuppa between meals.

I got the full English breakfast every morning: eggs, sausage, rashers, toast, marmalade and tea. Dinner—the noonday meal—was meat and three veg like roast lamb with mint sauce, cabbage, potato and peas, or haddock, chips and peas. Then the meal Tea, around 6 p.m.: soup, salad, bread. Dessert was apple pie with custard or strawberries and cream.

On market day, Hazel and I took the bus to Tavistock, Devon. Otherwise we walked. Hazel introduced me to the charm of the ten foot high hedgerows that flanked the narrow lanes. They are a little eco-system all to themselves and Hazel was acquainted with every creature that called the hedgerow home. She knew every flower, herb, and wort. I picked pimpernels, herb Robert, herb Bennet, marshmallow, and something she called catcia, and pressed them in a notebook.

We walked the mile and a half to Metherell to the family Baptist church. We walked the three miles to Cotehele House, the stately home of the Edgecumbe family. We walked the three miles to the Delaware school where Hazel had been a teacher and had the noonday meal in a cafe in the village of St Ann's Chapel. Hazel was certain I was famished that day because I hadn't eaten much for breakfast, meaning I had left the eggs off the full English breakfast.

We walked in the Combe to see the old Knott family home and Hazel pointed out the wall my great-great-great-grandfather, Mark, had built. "He was a small man," Hazel said. That was all anyone seemed to know about him, other than that he built the wall. Anytime his name was mentioned, someone told me. "Oh, yes, he was a small man."

I loved England and my Cornish family. It meant a great deal to me that I had made a good connection and had felt so welcome. We Americans are such a rootless bunch, the more so the farther west one goes. Coming from such a fractured family, the English connection was all the more poignant to me. Still my experience abroad was bewildering. I suppose that isn't unusual for a twenty-six-year-old but I think the thousand shocks the flesh is heir to don't have such rough edges when one has gotten a smoother start in life. Nothing was working quite like I imagined it would.

Mean to Me

"*WE ARE GATHERED HERE TODAY* in the face of this company, to join together Chuck and Mary in matrimony; which is an honorable and solemn estate and therefore is not to be entered into unadvisedly or lightly, but reverently and soberly."

"*Soberly* being the operative word," I thought as I stood first on one foot and then the other in the Olympia living room the day of my parents' remarriage.

My father had dried out; he had also decided that Mary was the only woman he could put up with. My mother had never considered marrying anyone else because she took a Catholic view of marriage: what God had joined together no man was to put asunder. She had lived with the shame of the divorce for nine years.

The day they decided to remarry, my father made a special call to tell me how excited he was.

"Do you want to come to a wedding?" he asked.

"Whose wedding?"

"Your mother and I are getting married again."

"Oh?" I knew I was expected to feel excited, but my parent's continual drama sucked the life out of me.

I was a reluctant witness on the license. Then I even more reluctantly had to hear my father's assessment of the wedding kiss.

"You know," he said to me privately. "When I kissed your mother just now, there was real passion!"

Oh my God, I did not want to hear about it. I was horrified. It should have been my wedding. Not to my father, of course, except . . . I was confused. I was stuck in an oedipal netherworld where I waited for my father to help my little girl crush resolve into a grown-up love affair with someone my age. Instead I lost a competition I didn't know I had registered for.

My parent's remarriage was something no one had seen coming. When I came home from Europe, they had been completely estranged. I had moved back into the house in the University district, was teaching in Head Start and trying to cope with their demands of me. My father had moved to Seattle where he drank heavily and had a series of lady friends. I stayed with him off and on when he was between women. He got drunk and sobbed every time I left him for a new adventure.

My mother had gotten into the habit of coming to Seattle unannounced. She expected me to drop everything and entertain her, as befitting someone who didn't exist apart from her. She walked into my house, passed my roommates and crawled into my bed, wanting me to get in with her and talk, something we had never done when I was growing up. The only time I got in bed with her was when I traded places with my father so I could sleep or when I was needed to squeeze the blackheads on her back, something I most assuredly was not doing now. These visits always ended badly, usually with me screaming at her and my mother sitting back smugly and saying wasn't I ashamed to act that way. It took me months to recover from her visits. Then she was back and we did it all over again.

She badgered me for news of her ex-husband. She was deeply ashamed to be divorced, yet she wore her martyrdom proudly. "*I* wasn't the one who wanted a divorce." She clung to this.

Or she persisted, "He was supposed to quit drinking." This, to her, was the only problem in her marriage.

"You're his favorite," she said to me. "You could get him to stop drinking."

I had been raised to think I was someone with special powers. This suited me because it helped me feel noticed and acknowledged. It provided me with a sense of who I was in the world. More than that, it kept me from knowing that the reason I felt so different from everyone else was because the grown-ups in my childhood had exploited, not protected, me. It kept me from realizing that I hadn't the faintest idea how to protect myself.

My father's apartment was in Leschi on the edge of Lake Washington. I checked on him daily on my way home from the Head Start center in Columbia City. I took meals to him and assessed how my magical powers were working on his alcoholism. Periodically I found vodka bottles and emptied them down the toilet. He laughed and bought more.

I worked the late shift at the Head Start center. I was the only adult on site when it was dark and the last child was picked up. My first night working late, I was waiting with three children when my father's car came creeping into the parking lot. I ran out to see what he wanted. He was drunk, completely soaked, the smell of it enough to knock me over.

"What are you doing here?" I was appalled.

"I came to make sure you were safe."

"You shouldn't be *driving! My God! Go home!*" I sobbed as I watched him wobble out the driveway at five miles an hour. But I had stuffed the dismay somewhere inside me by the time I got back to my charges.

One night I got a call from the Everett police. They had found my father wandering around Everett in a daze. I drove to Evergreen hospital, 30 minutes north of Seattle. My father couldn't remember anything that had happened.

"But I know that alcohol is involved somehow," he said, nodding his head sagely.

It scared him enough that he stopped drinking. My mother lost no time in marrying him again and he moved back to Olympia.

I didn't feel quite so responsible for him when he was sixty miles away. But inevitably, the day came when my mother called me to say that Chuck was drunk and she wanted me to come home.

I said, "Mom, if he's drinking, I don't want to know about it."

"But, but," she sputtered. "We are a family."

"Maybe," I said. "But this is your marriage and your problem. I'm done."

To her credit, she never again involved me in her worries about my father's drinking. The only intimations I had were the few occasions I smelled alcohol on him or noticed the early stages of inebriation, well remembered from my childhood. I have no idea how extensive his drinking was in his later life.

I got out of the alcoholism counseling business, but there was still plenty of family drama and I was years away from crafting a different family role for myself. The logic of my personality swirled around vague ideas about being good enough. If I was good enough, my father would stop drinking and my mother would be happy. I would finally get parents who loved me, noticed me, and gave me what I needed to put together my own life.

I invited my parents to a potluck for my 29th birthday. My mother exploded into the University district house with her salad fixings, and set about taking over the kitchen. Watching her tearing iceberg lettuce into a bowl, I reached in to pick out some of the many brown leaves.

"What are you doing?"

"Taking out the brown ones."

"They're perfectly good. My goodness, I didn't raise you to be wasteful."

"Nobody is going to eat them. You realize they are rotting?"

"They're perfectly good." She snatched them away from me.

One of my friends brought a beautiful romaine salad, the deep green of the leaves glistening with vinaigrette. When that bowl was empty and my mother's brown lettuce was left untouched, she erupted into the front room where we were all chewing away.

"*Why* is no one eating my salad?" she whined, piteously. Really it sometimes seemed like she was the drunk. I was mortified, but she wasn't done yet.

In an incident my physicist friends call "time coincident but not causal," I ran upstairs to get a sweater from my bedroom at the same time that my father was using the upstairs bathroom. When I came back downstairs, my mother gave me a hurt look. My roommate, Rosie, wouldn't look at me at all.

That evening, after everyone had gone home, I asked Rosie about the drama I had missed.

Rosie's face habitually wore a concerned expression. She hesitated, and then said, "Your mom wanted to know why you love your father better than her. She said the two of you were upstairs together and she wanted me to find out what you were doing."

I did not realize my mother was worried about my father's interest in me not because she thought he was molesting me, but because she was jealous of his attention. Certainly my father whom I was still calling by my pet name, Arthur, enjoyed both my idealization of him and the distress our relationship caused his wife. My parents had just remarried but I was still the drone in their repeated renditions of "Mean to Me."

Beyond that, my mother felt she ceased to exist when any attention was deflected from her to me, although she was pleased when my accomplishments could be co-opted for her enhancement. Psychically, she couldn't keep both of us in the same room at the same time. She couldn't acknowledge that I was there and I was not her.

Quite often, she hurled at me the unanswerable accusation that I loved my father more than I did her. There was no doubt that I preferred his company, but while I was in my twenties, I tried hard to understand my mother. Our stormy relationship was a continual source of distress and confusion to me. I needed a mother and I wanted to be close to my mother. I was still too young to understand that my mother's brain wiring made that impossible.

Whenever we approached some species of warmth and good feeling; suddenly my mother might scream, "Look how you're sitting! Do you sit like that around boys?" Or there would be some dire pronouncement about me not reading enough Bible. I would scroll back through the conversation, trying to figure out why I deserved the assault.

The accusation that I loved my father more than her had a twin: "You don't care anything about my family."

"You never want to talk about your family," I protested.

"Well, there isn't much to say. We worked hard. We didn't have anything."

"Did my grandmother bring recipes from the old country? Do you know any Bulgarian folk songs?"

"They are all sad. We were sad. We didn't have all the stuff you kids have. My goodness! You don't know the value of anything"

"How many instruments did Alec play? Did he sing?"

"You don't really want to know."

I knew the story of her idealized brother, Alec who was murdered because people were jealous of his talents, and not because he and his drunken buddies had gotten careless with a shotgun.

Another Kiosse story explained a great deal about my mother, and through her legacy, me. When they married each other, my grandparents, Georg and Elena, had children from previous marriages. Together they had something like twelve children, two of whom were born in what was then Bessarabia, and seven of whom survived out in eastern Montana. When Georg made the decision to leave the Balkans in 1914, Elena was forced, whether by Georg or the in-laws or by other forces, to leave behind three of her children, all under the age of ten.

"God is punishing me for leaving behind my children," was her response to tragedies and hardships for the rest of her life.

Of the many unfortunate repercussions for this belief, its burden on the children she didn't leave behind seems the most pernicious. My mother once told me that a daughter's job was to do everything she could to help her mother, including, I presume, make up for the loss and tragedy that is part of life.

But by my late twenties, I had lost track of why I was doing anything. It was just what one did. People had parents and families that kept in touch and spent holidays together. Family was the default place to be. It was The Way Life Is. The fact that it could take me weeks to recover from an afternoon spent with my parents didn't lessen my obligation to love them and be with them. I believed this even without the Christian community reinforcing it.

Years later, when I told my therapist that my mother thought a daughter's job was to do everything she could for her mother, he commented dryly, "You did."

Mai

EIGHTEEN-YEAR-OLD *MAI LA WALKED* off the plane at SeaTac airport wearing her little Chinese pajamas and blinking in the harsh lights. I didn't need the photo I had gotten from World Relief to help me identify her. No one else was wearing pajamas and no one else looked so scared. Mai was coming to live with me after escaping from South Vietnam and spending 18 months in refugee camps in Malaysia. A casualty of the endless Vietnam War, Mai was one of the "boat people" who were arriving in masses on the American west coast.

I watched the situation from the side lines for a while but I was impatient with the limitations of social services. I was living in a big house with a bedroom large enough for two beds. I wanted to sponsor someone who would live with me: a single woman or a woman with a baby. Three months later, Mai La arrived in Seattle. A Chinese friend accompanied me to the airport to act as translator. Nghiem took us to his home, and cooked dinner for us. Between the two of them they knew about six languages and they managed to find one with which to communicate.

Later on the drive to my house, Mai asked in careful English, "What is your name?" It was the first thing she said directly to me. We were complete strangers who would live together for two years.

That night I showed her how to get under the covers of an American bed, and we fell asleep in the same room. Thus began a wonderful adventure. Rosie and the rest of the household rose to the occasion. We took Mai shopping and sightseeing. We helped her with English. We tried to learn Chinese. Whenever she left the house, she carried a card with her address, phone number, bus number and a few phrases she might need: "I am lost." or "Where is the rest room?" "Where is Bus 75?" We got used to the smell of garlic and fish being cooked first thing in the morning and the bathroom being periodically steamed up from hand laundry.

Children of emotionally disturbed parents are used to being weighted down with the needs of people who won't help themselves; and of feeling messianic about their abilities to save. Messiahs always get crucified. Martyrdom becomes a badge of honor because it's all one has got left. Those were already my patterns, but they were misplaced with Mai. She not only took responsibility for herself, but she had love to give.

While I was fussing about how to enroll her in a school, she quietly found her way into Roosevelt High School where she completed an ESL course and got her high school diploma. In the midst of similar hyperventilations about finding her a job, she came home with a W4 form and a job in a local photography studio. Anyone who has had a portrait taken at Seattle's Yuen Lui photography studio in the last 25 years may have Mai to thank for taking out his pimples or smoothing her wrinkles.

One night I woke myself up, sobbing. I don't remember what I was dreaming but it was bound to be about either Andy or my parents. In seconds, two arms were around me and a body was pressed up against mine in my bed. When I think about Mai, I often think of the swiftness of those two arms around me and that there was no need for words. She offered a comfort I had little acquaintance with.

Hopelessly Devoted

I DIDN'T KNOW WHERE THE SINGER in me had gone. The desire was there but so was the fear. I made some progress with a teacher at Cornish Institute. Julie was always dieting and always hungry so she sucked hard candies at my lessons. After my lessons, she gathered up all the little pieces of cellophane wrappers that had blown onto the floor. After a few years, she left for New York City and I never heard what happened to her.

When I was 30 I found a teacher, Lester McCall, a temperamental redhead who informed me that he was the best teacher in Seattle. I took his boasting with a grain of salt at first. But under the spell of his gigantic ego, I began to believe he had special powers.

I learned to expand my rib cage when I breathed and to maintain expansion when I sang. I had a large lung capacity and could sing long phrases easily. I learned to open my throat in a yawn and enormous round sounds would pop out. I found I had a flexible voice that could race all the way up to A-flat above high C. I tore through repertoire. I sang light coloratura, all the bird song literature, Handel, Mozart, Schubert, Bach, Rossini and loved it all.

My parents were thrilled. They knew I loved to sing and they remembered how miserable I had been when the vocal nodule stopped my voice. But emotionally needy parents need to have extraordinary children to buttress their self-esteem. My brother, Alex, had moved to Seattle and was making a living as a potter. His pots had a classic simplicity. He favored subtle earth tones with a hint of parabola sketched across the surface. My parents were immensely proud of Alex, but I had not done much for them in that department lately.

I went to Olympia to sing "Una voce poco fa" and "Lo hear the gentle lark." They smiled and nodded.

My mother said, "Now sing 'The Old Rugged Cross.'"

There's no doubt that Lester coaxed a voice out of me that I didn't know I had, but I had little vocal stamina. I could sing at a lesson and that usually set me up so that I could sing a bit more that day, but then I would have laryngitis of the high notes. Sounds wouldn't come out. It had been this way since I had the vocal nodules. Most singers I knew, once they were warmed up, they could go for hours. Once I was warmed up, the clock was ticking. I only had an hour's voice on my own, maybe two hours if I had warmed up with Lester. I tried to talk to him about this

"It doesn't happen when I warm you up?"

"Not as much."

"Well, that tells you something, doesn't it?"

"But I don't know what I am doing wrong."

"Well, I'm not doing it to you."

Was that the prime consideration here? It was like talking to my mother.

In addition to the anxiety about whether or not my voice would be there when I opened my mouth, I was anxious—as all performers are— about making mistakes.

"I don't want you singing anywhere except church until you can keep your wits about you. When you sing in public, it's a reflection on me," he told me. "There's no getting around that."

I resented this, but it was familiar territory.

Lester suggested I work on a recital to be performed in Olympia "where all your support is." He didn't add that it was a venue where no one knew him, but that was understood. I didn't tell him that none of my support was in Olympia. I rarely contradicted him and he rarely asked me what I thought or wanted.

He chose all the music and micro-managed every detail of the recital. When I showed him a copy of the program I had made, he told me my bio should address me as Miss Richmond, not Elena. As in "Miss

Richmond is a student of Lester McCall." Or: "Miss Richmond's ego shrinks to the size of a raisin in order to squeeze in the door of Lester McCall's music studio."

I sang a dress rehearsal in Seattle for a wildly enthusiastic group of friends and acquaintances from church. This was a surprise on several levels. First, I always underestimated the amount of love that was available to me. And secondly, I sang better because of it.

My mother, meantime, was in her element, arranging to have me reflect on her as a mother. Her friend, Lillian, who had a lovely old home and a grand piano, offered her living room. I was bringing an accomplished accompanist, Lisa Bergman, from Seattle. I had Lillian's piano tuned. My mother got together all her friends plus my high school piano teacher, now in a wheelchair, suffering from various consequences of diabetes. All I remember of the audience of 50 people, was Jane, slumped over in her wheelchair, her eyesight almost gone; still listening, still hearing.

I spent the night before the recital at my parent's home. My mother surprised me with a peach-colored dress she had made and fitted to her body, intending me to wear it when I sang. I reluctantly tried it on. The style made my breasts look like I had a big sausage stretched across my chest. The collar and armhole facings stuck out, making me look like a giant pastel pixie.

"I'm not wearing this," I said.

"Of course you are," my mother said. "I made it for you to wear. You'll have to tack the facing."

I was awake most of the night, angry and anxious. In the morning I found enough nerve to tell my mother in a shaking voice that needed to sing later in the day, "I am not your paper doll. I brought my own dress."

I wore my own dress and tried to block my mother's hurt look from my mind. I tried to block her interferences altogether. When she pestered Lester to have me sing *The Lord's Prayer* as an encore, I walked out of the room, leaving him to cope with her.

I sang the recital. I sang Handel, Faure, and Schubert in schoolgirl Italian, French, and German. I sang "The Trees on the Mountain" from *Susannah* and "Lucy's Aria" from *The Telephone*. I sang songs I had worked on until I was sick to death of them. Lester had drawn blood out of me in our years of work on "Una Voce Poco Fa" from *The Barber of Seville*. And Schubert's "Seligkeit."

"It's a song about how wonderful it is to be in love," Lester stormed at me. "Why can't you sing it that way?"

I was nervous but for a first recital, I believe it was a good attempt. Afterwards Lillian put her hand on my arm and gushed about how beautiful my voice was and what courage I had. "Now, if you could just lose some weight, you'd be so lovely."

Lovely or not, an odd thing started to happen after that recital. I got to my lesson at 11:00 a.m. I knocked, and then pounded on the door. Lester was in his pajamas when he opened it. He went to the bathroom for 15 minutes and finally we began the lesson. He spent my lesson time talking about his personal life, his ex-wife, his physical ailments, his tax problems, and about his many successful students. I heard the same stories over and over while I stood there ready to start the warm-up.

Once, prior to a performance, he told a joke, the punch line of which required him to come close to me, stare at my breasts and say "If only those were brains." He laughed. I went numb. I sang very badly that night. By the end of the evening, Lester was annoyed and I was the one who felt ashamed when of course, it ought to have been the other way around.

He wanted me to come for lessons twice a week but since I couldn't pay for them, he waived the fee. This set up a feeling of indebtedness accompanied by an anxiety that I didn't understand. Lester didn't drive, either because of his medications or because he was just generally unstable. I started chauffeuring him around town and running errands for him. I catalogued all his music for him. This required me to sit for hours in his stuffy, dank bedroom where all his scores were heaped in boxes.

I started to feel sexually attracted and this made my anxiety unbearable. I was 30 years old. He was 60. He had deplorable personal habits. He smelled like urine. I didn't know why I had sexual feelings, but since he felt rather like my father –except that my father smelled like Old Spice—I thought everything was probably okay. I thought this was a normal state of affairs in loving relationships. No child can afford to know her parents are exploiting her and calling it love. I was still very much a child.

My anxiety boiled over one day when stuck close together in a car, Lester told me about a music teacher who had married his student 40 years younger than himself. He leered at me and I broke out into a cold sweat. Did he think that was where we were headed? I told him I wasn't interested in men and he shrank to his side of the car.

I had no one to talk to. I went, of all places, to my parents. This is what people do, right? This is what parents are for. My mother, uncharacteristically, said nothing.

My father said, "Well, you are going to have lots of experiences like this in life. Just don't disappoint him in your singing after all he has put into you."

I sang Lucy's Aria from *The Telephone* in my first big contest. It had a high D at the end. Beyond Lisa, my accompanist, I had no support. No friends cheering me on. Lester didn't want to be there. I didn't want him to be there. It was just as well that he wasn't there because the high note didn't come out. I was uncomfortable on the stage. I had no training to do other than stand rooted like a tree and sing with a pretty voice. I was anxious about being seen, anxious that I "stuck out too much." With so little permission to be human, tension built in my body as I sang. I couldn't pop that D out at the end.

When Lester called me that evening to find out how it had gone, I tried to make a joke of it, "Oh well, the D didn't quite come out but I dropped the telephone at the same time so I think it looked like part of the act."

"What do you mean you dropped the telephone? You had a prop? Did I tell you to have a prop? You think this is a joke? When you sing in public I expect you to be prepared and to keep your wits about you. People *know* you are my student. You will never be a singer because you don't take your singing seriously. This wasn't some little church service. No more contests!"

For a full five minutes he went on in this vein while I stood, stunned, holding the phone to my ear. I was awake all that night, levitating with anxiety. I had had enough. I had the name of a therapist. In the morning, I called his number and set up my first appointment.

Symphony Pathétique

I KNEW ABOUT DOUG FROM A CLASS he taught called "Becoming Peers with your Parents," aiming to help people find space from their family of origin. He was the son of an evangelical minister; we could both quote long passages of scripture and we knew the same gruesome hymns. An MSW, he worked with object relations and family-of-origin theory and had a special interest in grief, loss, and attachment theory. As a social worker in the emergency department of a big hospital, his skill with crisis and drama would come in handy when working with me. He shook my hand when we first met. For the next 25 years, though we were involved in a deeply intimate undertaking, we never again touched.

Doug was reserved but had a wry sense of humor that I loved. He wore casual clothes in flamboyant colors. He had a pair of brick red jeans and another of canary yellow. His hair, which was rapidly receding, was in a curly permanent and he had braces on his teeth. He was tall and big, an athlete. On his desk, where he could easily see it, was a postcard from the movie *Stop Making Sense*. He drove a VW Rabbit. He was five years older than me and our birthdays were two days apart. In 1985, Doug's fee was $30 an hour. He had been doing therapy for about a year.

He asked me if I minded if he took notes. But within 10 minutes, the clipboard had slipped to the floor, his eyes on my face. And I, for the second time in my life, felt like someone was listening.

I looked forward to my sessions. Doug's inclinations were toward the psychoanalytic. I wasn't entirely sure what that was, but it suited me. There were no goals, no direction, no homework, and no advice. There was no obvious technique. He told me I could say anything I wanted to say. We talked about my childhood, my parents, Christianity, Andy, Lester, and my decision to teach private music lessons as a way to support myself while I pursued a career in singing.

We talked about my body. I hardly knew I had one. I had fainted during my first pelvic exam. I managed to buy a copy of *Our Bodies, Ourselves* and a hand mirror. After three false starts, I made it into Bartell Drugs to buy some K-Y jelly. I learned how to give myself an orgasm. The first time I came, I laughed out loud. I discovered the versatility of zucchini. I had progressed a little from "only married women can use tampons."

One session, about two years into therapy, we talked about my father. "You called him Arthur?"

"It was just a joke. In your class, you suggested that we try calling our parents by their first names."

"But his name wasn't Arthur. When you called him Arthur, he felt like your boyfriend, not your father."

"So?"

"When you began to develop sexually, you needed him to affirm your sexuality as your father, not as your boyfriend. It was natural for you to want your father but he needed to remember that he was married to your mother. Instead he dangled the possibility that your fantasy might work out, that you could have him all to yourself."

There was a long pause. I felt defensive. "It was just a joke," I repeated.

Doug commented, "You had your father to yourself but you aren't able to have me."

I stared at him. Something terrifying was getting too close. "What makes you think I want *you*?"

An hour after I left the office, I had a panic attack. Up until then I had lived with high levels of anxiety but this was something different. My heart pounded like it was going to blow open my rib cage, my knees buckled, and my mind whited out. I felt like my insides were turning to liquid and I was about to spill out onto the floor. I found myself in the produce section of Larry's Market with no idea how I had gotten there. I looked around and wondered why no one was rushing over to help. I thought I was dying.

It was an episode that spent itself in about an hour, leaving me shaken and exhausted. But it happened again that night. It happened repeatedly for three days. I resisted the urge to call Doug because I was terrified of the deepening transference. My fears about my father had run like an electrical line through interactions with the men I had dated thus far. Now my fears about my father were infiltrating my good feelings about Doug.

After three days of panic episodes, I finally let myself call Doug. He listened for a long time and asked a few questions. His breathing sounded very loud like it sometimes can over the phone and I found this comforting. He asked me if there was someplace I could go where I would be able to sleep and to feel safe. I was horrified that beyond that, he didn't tell me what to do.

In my next session, I erupted. "You *gave* me too much last time," I stormed at him. "It's your fault that this happened! I never had panic attacks before I started talking to you!"

A great ball of rage came screeching out of me and I grabbed the Kleenex box and slammed it to the floor. I pulled at my hair so ferociously that my clips came out. I beat on the chair arm and the window ledge until the force of it made my shoes fly off my feet. One of them landed next to Doug's chair. He moved it to the side, his eyes on me. I screamed with rage so intense I could hardly stuff it into words fast enough to spit out. Then I sobbed. Finally, I stared at the Kleenex box and breathed hard.

Years later when we talked about this incident, I claimed to not have been aiming the Kleenex box at him. Doug disagreed. He told me that he was afraid of me at times. It was still early in his career and my transference was a bit of a surprise; not the concept itself, but the force of my feelings.

I started having panic attacks a lot. The neighbor's stereo, thumping through the walls, would set one off. Soon just the sound of the neighbor coming home would trigger an attack. I was living by myself in an old house near Green Lake that had been partitioned into three apartments. Negotiations with the neighbors over noise resulted in my going up the street to a church to practice my singing, but not with any concessions on their part.

One night they had a huge party. I called the police who were kind to me and diffused the situation. But the next morning, things were openly hostile. I was terrified of my neighbors because I knew I was at their mercy. They blasted their music just to torment me. They bought a set of drums and banged on them when my piano students came. They gunned their car engines and screeched by my front door, yelling obscenities at me.

It was one thing for there to be a noise problem to negotiate. It was another when a sadistic hostility was paired with it. The panic attacks were a way of not thinking: not thinking about the emotional intrusion of my father sitting on my bed, drunk, and complaining about his marriage; not thinking that my mother's anxiety had carved out my personality with little accommodation for what dreams and desires I had; not thinking that their pre-occupation with each other meant that I had not felt noticed, let alone loved. When I heard the thump of the stereo, the monolithic structure in my mind that represented The Unthinkable would loom out of its foggy swamp and come too close. I panicked because I couldn't think. I couldn't think because it frightened me and because it hurt too much.

When I wasn't panicking, I felt suicidal. The two states were self-correcting, and I swung back and forth. I started a tricyclic anti-depressant, Doxepin, which didn't eliminate either state, just sedated me so their effects weren't so intense. When the depression or the panic felt intolerable, I called Doug. He had given me his home phone number and his phone number at the hospital. I called him several times a week. Sometimes I sobbed over the phone, sometimes I raged at him. Sometimes it helped; sometimes it made me feel worse. Talking to Doug was like a drug: sometimes it was a good high, sometimes a bad trip.

Sometimes when I felt raw, when I felt something wild clawing at the inside of my rib cage, I went driving on the country roads in Snohomish County. I drove very fast, drove without thinking, sometimes without having the least idea where I was. I liked the hum of the car, and the feel of the road coming toward me, going under me and slipping behind me. I liked the feeling that I wasn't anywhere in particular. I was en route. Sometimes when I couldn't sleep, even with a sedating drug in me, I went out after midnight, in my nightgown, and drove until two or three in the morning. I drove until the wild feeling subsided. I'd think, "OK, I'm done. That's enough." Then I'd figure out where I was and drive home.

I tried to talk to my parents about what was happening inside me. Their best line was always: "It doesn't do any good to dwell on the past." My mother showed up with a bag full of books from the 1950s. The title on top was *Jesus and Mental Health.* I dropped the bag in the garbage.

My father decided my weight was all that was wrong with me. He sent me a letter, written as dialectic, an imaginary conversation between the two of us, wherein he provided all my responses to his questions about how he had lost eight pounds by increasing the time spent on his stationery bicycle and leaving the nuts off his nightly portion of ice cream. His final condescension sounded like something out of *Woman's Day* magazine, "If you will keep your hand out of the cookie jar, I will buy you a stationary bike."

I tore the letter into little pieces. Then I taped them back together and wrote "Fuck you" and "Asshole" all over it. I wanted to rage at him but I was afraid to. My father didn't fight back, he coldly disappeared.

I obsessed about my weight which fluctuated from between 20 and 50 pounds more than I thought it should be. Since I viewed my weight as a character defect, it was a continual source of humiliation for me. After my friend, Mandy, asked me to be her maid of honor, her mother made sure I learned that she objected to her daughter's choice. I was so fat I would ruin the wedding photo, she said.

In those days, I always lied about what size I wore. As a result, the bridesmaid's dress was so tight you could have bounced a quarter off it. Mortified, I went on a near starvation diet. At the same time, the dress was sent to be let out. On Mandy's wedding day, I had to be pinned into the dress because it was now too big. Months later, Mandy sent me a lovely photo of just the two of us in our wedding day attire, my elbows pressed against my sides to obscure any odd bulges where the fabric had been hurriedly taken in.

People in the helping professions had varying degrees of tact when they mentioned my weight, but they always said something and I always seethed in silent rage and shame. I fired one of my doctors over an interaction about my weight. I went to see her because I had a spasm in my upper back. But she wanted to talk about my weight because women's nutrition was her specialty.

"I know quite a bit about nutrition," I said. "That isn't my problem."

It was as though I hadn't spoken. "I want you to keep a food diary," she said, handing me a special chart she had designed herself. "And come back next week."

"But I came in for a steroid shot in my upper back," I said

"I don't have time to do that today because we talked about this other thing," she said cheerfully.

Today, I can't imagine being in the fearful mental space that bred what I did next: I took her special chart home and choking on my own rage, I filled it out in exquisite, sarcastic detail, right down to the color of the last M&M. She was The Doctor and at that point I wouldn't have dreamt of non-compliance.

My second appointment for the spasm in my upper back was taken up with a lecture about the M&Ms and a referral to see a nutritionist.

"You don't have an eating disorder," she told me. "You don't have emotional issues around food. You just need some nutritional education."

That was my limit. I tore the referral up in front of her. "You are not listening to me," I said. "And you don't know anything about me."

I marched out and wrote her a letter. I read the letter to Doug who by this time had seen me through half a dozen doctors. "She needed some feedback!" I declared.

"Not from you," he said wearily.

Finding my primal rage had been a great break-though, but I didn't know how to contain it. Doug was still new enough to his profession that he wasn't quite sure what to do with me either.

In addition to the weight problems, the depression and anxiety, I had arthritis in my back and continual dental drama. My teeth were going down like dominoes, one abscess after another, necessitating seven root canals, all of them emergencies because nothing ever showed up on an x-ray. I could diagnose an abscess better than the dentists.

"Please, just open it up and start a root canal!" I'd beg.

"But there's no evidence that we need to do that," they'd say and send me home with no pain meds.

I'd be back the next day for an emergency appointment. Then the teeth needed to be crowned and I ended up having five of them extracted after all.

I struggled on. As difficult as physical activity was, I tried to get exercise. I liked taking walks in Carkeek Park, a kind of wild preserve near my house. But my back would regularly flare up so that I couldn't do anything but move very slowly from bed to chair. It was discouraging at best. At worst, I excoriated myself for being a Big. Fat. Lazy. Slobby. Sexless. Block of Wood.

I was still hanging out with Christians, still imagining this was where I would find acceptance and value. The Church was a replacement womb, not as harsh as my mother's mind but still in a familiar neighborhood. But the Christians I knew weren't equipped to understand me. Nor did anyone have the time: I was pretty much a full time job. Many of them were of the opinion that Christians had no business needing a therapist. They were sure that Jesus was the answer but they didn't want to hear any of my questions.

The one friend who mattered was Juliet, the woman who had written such sympathetic letters to me when I was homesick in France. She was the kindest person I had ever known. She had a beautiful face and eyes that laughed when she smiled. Her subtle sense of humor expressed an appreciation for the absurdity of life. Bright and courageous, she hadn't much confidence in herself in those years. We had both been raised by deeply religious parents; we called her missionary parents "professional Christians."

We were moving at comparable speeds towards the exit ramp from evangelical Christianity, gaining momentum as well as jokes from each other. I thought it was screamingly funny to sing hymns that used the word "come" while decidedly erotic pictures went through my head: "Come, Thou Long Expected," and "O Come all Ye Faithful." "Come Thou Fount" was an especially juicy text because it had that verse that begins: "Here I raise my Ebenezer, hither by thy help I'm come." For pure kinesthetic pulsations, the winner was always the Church in the Wildwood with its thumping chorus: "Come, come, come, come, come to the church in the wild wood." One would have to know firsthand the terror of hell-based Christianity to understand both how sacrilegious and how liberating it was to translate those hymns into the language of sex.

I was still sexually inexperienced. Juliet who was going through a divorce, looked at my cartoon book called *Why Do I Need a Man when I have a Cucumber*, and inspected the size of the zucchinis I was buying.

"Someday, Elena," she said, "I think you're going to be very disappointed."

Juliet lived near the University while she worked on her master's degree. I bicycled across town and we spent afternoons talking, working on projects, going out for coffee, shopping. Later when she got a teaching position, Juliet always had paperwork to do so we rode the Seattle ferries back and forth across Puget Sound while she worked and I wrote. Occasionally we shared holiday celebrations. When I had gall bladder surgery, Juliet picked me up at the hospital and I spent two nights with her before I went home.

She complained once, "We always do what you want to do. It's never what I want."

I asked, "What do you want to do then? Let's do it."

She wanted to go hiking. So we went hiking.

That might have been a clue that the friendship was imbalanced. This is the way someone talks when she doesn't realize she has rights, when she is expecting someone else to confer value on her. I was doing the same thing with Doug. Lost in my transference, I thought that he was conferring value on me. I suggested Juliet consult with him. That suggestion was going to create trouble.

Hell Freezes Over

A LOT OF THINGS HAPPENED IN THE SPRING of my 37th year. For three, I got dry skin, wrinkles around my eyes, and patches of grey hair. And I stopped my lessons with Lester. It took a year of therapy before I was even able to consider the idea that there might be better teachers for me.

Lester was old school. He was the Maestro to be obeyed, not questioned. Every step of the way, he expected me to do what I was told and he threw fits when I asserted something of myself. I truly believed what he believed about himself: that he was best teacher in town and for me to go anywhere else would be a huge mistake.

But I had pursued acting classes and consulted with coaches on my stage presence and interpretation of arias. I wanted to know what to do with my body and my hands. Lester was offended. He sulked. He declared that he would teach me what I needed to know; anything else wasn't important. I was in the well-known territory of not feeling like I could leave Lester until I had some unknown Thing that only he could give me. Only when he pronounced me a singer would I be a Singer.

One of our last battles was over his insistence that I learn to interpret a song by first getting a mental image or as he put it: "Have a mental picture in your mind." Then he quizzed me about the image so he could approve it.

Driving during a snowstorm, I listened to Kiri Te Kanawa sing "Let the bright Seraphim." Flakes whirled and danced in patterns that were so compelling, I pulled over so I could listen and watch. I was working on the aria at the time and the dancing snowflakes became my mental image. It gave the piece the buoyancy I felt it needed.

At my next lesson, the conversation went like this:

"What is the mental picture in your mind?"

"Well, I was driving the other day in the snowstorm—"

"No!" he interrupted. "There's no snow in heaven."

I looked at him in astonishment. "How do you know?"

"Don't answer back!"

"You want me to have my own interpretations. How can I do that if I have to use your ideas?"

He laughed uncomfortably. "Well, that's the thing."

"What does that mean?"

"My dear, you must stop fighting me."

We had a huge fight the day I told him I was leaving. Lester was furious.

"You, my dear, have not behaved like a lady," he fumed. "You are ungrateful and will never be a singer because you can't take criticism." He wagged his finger at me. "You couldn't sing "Happy Birthday" when you came to me."

"Don't you *dare* shake your finger in my face," I hissed at him. I was amazed at my audacity and amazed when he actually put his hand down.

"I *am* a singer," I declared. "I would have learned to sing with any teacher because I *wanted* to learn to sing."

I wasn't actually sure of this; it was something unexpected that popped out of me from somewhere deep inside.

I slammed the door on my way out of his studio.

Wandering the Mandela

THE OTHER BIG DECISION OF THAT SPRING was to buy a house. I had come to the conclusion that while I couldn't tolerate other people's noise, I needed to be able to make my own. I needed a house with a big yard and lots of space between me and my neighbors. This was actually rather a radical idea in the 80's. Single women didn't buy homes of their own. They rented apartments until they got married.

My parents helped with the down payment and were thrilled to do so, even my mother who was famous for saying, "We are not giving you kids any more money until you learn how to spend it!" and who was worried that if I owned a house, I would never find a husband. I was grateful to my parents for the financial help. They had been of such little help in so many other ways, I felt fortunate that their desire to help me financially lined up with something that I actually wanted.

I became a gardener. I didn't have a plan; it was a grand experiment. If a plant wasn't flourishing, I learned to move it around or water it more or less and see what it responded to. The best piece of gardening advice I ever got came from a character in *Staying On*, Paul Scott's sequel to *The Raj Quartet*. The mali counsels that all living things need space to breathe. Whenever I was perplexed about a plant, I considered if there was something I could do that would help it breathe. It was good advice for gardening, for singing, and for life.

I set up my music studio overlooking the garden of my new house. I took out a wall so the studio could open into the front room. For recitals I seated the audience in the front room and used the studio as a stage. I had by this time, been teaching private piano lessons for several years and all my students were coming by referral. I had a waiting list and I worked as much as my energy allowed.

I could be having a full blown panic attack at 3:30 when my first student came up the walk but by the time we sat down at the piano, I would have stuffed it somewhere until I was alone again. I credit this ability to hide myself as causing some of my problems in the first place but it also kept me out of the psych ward. I had learned from an alcoholic father and a disturbed mother who kept their craziness private, to never miss a day of work.

I loved teaching. I had an intuitive way of working with the children who came for lessons. I had never forgotten what it felt like to be a child: the wonder and curiosity; also the confusion, the fear of adults, and the feelings of powerlessness. At their first lesson, I wrote my name and phone number in their assignment books and told them they could call me if they forgot what to do or hated the music or didn't want to practice or for any reason at all. I removed the parents from anything except paying my fee. I didn't want to deal with any parents. They were usually glad to be off the hook for enforcing practicing at home and my students stayed with me for years.

I didn't have a degree in music. My major at Whitman had been English literature. I had also gotten an education certificate because my mother wanted me to be a first grade teacher like she was. In addition I needed Something to Fall Back On when everything I desired turned out to have been worthless and when I learned that Mother Knew Best after all. I had been practically eaten alive teaching junior high for one semester in the public school system, and then I had let the certificate lapse.

I decided to become certified through the National Music Teachers Association. This required me to take a theory exam, a music history exam and to play a program for a jury. In preparation I studied Edith Borroff's music history textbook like I had once studied *Knowing God*. I read it through three times, took enough notes, and made enough outlines to reproduce the book itself.

To prepare for the theory exam, I enrolled in a music theory course at the University of Washington. I expected something along the lines of what I had done at Whitman which was a programmed workbook. But Ken Benshoof taught theory by having us write and arrange music. There was no text. As a bonus, he said funny things in class like, "Now these chords were used a lot in early church music because they have no hormones."

I asked Dr Benshoof for his office hours. It had been fifteen years since I had studied music theory. I felt rusty and had questions.

"Ask me in class," he advised. "If you have questions, there are others who have the same questions. Or if they have other questions, they need to speak up."

This was an unexpected response. I felt both respected and drawn into the process.

One day I asked a question about an augmented 6th chord I was working with. Dr Benshoof answered me with a question: "How are you spelling it?" From my spelling, he fashioned an answer to my question.

This small interaction expanded into a big idea. Every question—about anything, not just music theory—could be a door into a whole world of possibilities, all of them mediated by the mind that asked the question and the mind that answered. I became curious about what was going on in my students' minds and I tried to use their conceptions and ideas as an exploratory starting point. Learning became a ramble around a colorful, complex mandala where perceptions shifted and ideas migrated. This appealed to me so much more than filling in the blanks of a programmed text. It solved the conundrum of which is louder, a bee or a doorbell.

Another big idea grew from an assignment to write an arrangement of "Rudolph, the Red Nosed Reindeer. " One of my classmates asked Dr. Benshoof how he would arrange it. It was a smart aleck question designed to find out the Right Answer. Dr. Benshoof had a robust bullshit meter, but his answer surprised me. "I wouldn't," he said. "I have no reason to arrange this song. I don't want to arrange it."

Here was something about desire. From the desire to arrange the song would flow ideas about how to arrange it. When the desire is simply to pass the music class, the arrangement of the song is going to be uninspiring. I despise the song "Rudolph the Red-Nosed Reindeer" so I didn't particularly *want* this assignment. But I wanted to see what kind of fun I could have with my arrangement. I diddled with the tune and the words; put in some trademark sarcasm, and some incongruous churchy harmonies. I enjoyed creating my version. I still hate the song.

After two semesters with Kenneth Benshoof, all of my teaching ideas re-ordered themselves. I learned to have five different ways of answering a question or working with a learning problem, beginning with finding out how the student was conceptualizing the material. "How are you spelling it?" I would think when a student asked a question. That was code for "Find out what this student is thinking." Or more often, because I was working with children, I recognized that they were too confused to even ask a question. So I'd say, "Ok, tell me everything you can about what you see on this page." And we'd go from there.

Max was a 6-year-old who told me, "Well…the two line songs are too short and the four line songs are just too long." He folded his hands in his lap and heaved a considerable sigh. "I just can't do this."

I glanced over at his mother. She shrugged and went back to her book. I loved the parents who shrugged and went back to their books, leaving me to do my job. They were the only ones I allowed to sit in on lessons.

I looked at Max who was gazing disinterestedly out the window. My other code phrase was "What does this child want?" I went fishing to find out.

"OK," I said. "Pick any three lines you want to play, any lines in the whole book, they don't even have to be from the same song or on the same page."

He considered this for a few minutes and then said, "I think I could play four lines if you don't stop me."

This was what was really bothering him, what he couldn't verbalize: I interrupted him too much. Once he started to play, he wanted to play to the end, then go back and fix the mistakes.

Another little guy, Hunter, came back playing "The Lighthouse Gleams, Beware!" so badly I hardly knew where to start. He had left out all the sharps. There had been no rhythm, just notes played at whatever point he played them. Some of his fingering involved turning his hand over and using his knuckles. It was one big mess, like a finger painting.

I sat still for a few seconds, thinking. Finally I said, "Well, what do you think of the way you played this?"

He smiled his charming little-boy smile. He was clearly in love with life. "I think it was pretty good!" he said cheerfully.

I smiled my charming teacher smile and chose one thing to have him try differently. He set out to master the two F-sharps with great interest and curiosity. "It sure sounds better that way," he commented.

He played all the F sharps on the piano. He played "The Lighthouse Gleams, Beware!" in every octave of the piano. Then we worked on the knuckle business.

In lessons with me, learning was circuitous, but I was delighted with the way it worked. Students figured out their own reasons why it might be good to learn a few scales or do finger exercises. This removed a lot of resistance to what is historically the bane of piano practice. When I didn't force anything, my students got curious about the many different kinds of music they might be able to play. I loved it when the most world-weary, jaded adolescent, reeking of grape bubble gum, with black nail polish and green streaks in her hair, set aside her pop idol du jour and told me she thought Bach was cool and was there something of his that wasn't too hard for her?

I became a better teacher when I started paying attention to my students' desires. When I thought of their minds as maps showing places I hadn't been, with tentative new roads we would attempt to travel together. I was confident that though I was the teacher, they would show me how to help them learn music. I was confident that no matter how we traveled or how often we might stall or get lost, no matter how much a parent might try to backseat drive, in the end, my students would learn as much or as little music as they wanted.

While there can be complex and competing desires, Desire itself, can be clarifying. I believe we only do what we truly want to do. We only learn when we feel safe enough to loosen our hold on rigid beliefs. If we have enough freedom to sit where we are without judgment or fear, we can start to find other places to be. This was psychoanalytic at its core and miles away from the pronouncements of the gang at College Life Christian Fellowship, Rick, or more to the point, my mother.

It was still miles away from my emotional difficulties, too, but slowly I was learning to let unconscious processes loosen the constrictions of my own mind. Now when I read a book like *Knowing God* or Edith Borroff's music history text, or when I took a class, I was not bent over a notebook scribbling furiously, trying to take down every word that might unlock the meaning of life if I could just digest it, maybe next week after the holidays were over and after finishing my taxes, and if I could remember where I put the notebook. I began to enjoy the experience of learning, confident that my mind would remember what was immediately important—the door into the mandela—and would serve up later relevancies later. I had an image of ideas floating around like so much fluff. Some of that fluff would stick to me and that would be enough for the present.

I wrote my certification thesis about student-centered teaching. I was exuberant about individualized ways of teaching, taking the time to let students formulate their own questions and find their own circuitous route through the learning process to find the path with the greatest joy and fascination for them. I received glowing comments from one of the adjudicators and a big sour grimace from another.

She looked me up and down and said, "I did things differently once. Never again."

I finished the history and theory exams with high marks but tanked on the jury. I had not enjoyed preparing for the performance, had not slept well the night before, and had terrible stage fright that day. I played reasonably well the four Bach inventions and sinfonias, two Chopin mazurkas, and two Bartok Bulgarian Dances. But I fell apart on the Beethoven Sonata. As I launched into the first movement, I thought to myself: "I am never playing this piece ever again." So not an auspicious beginning. The Dragon Lady decided that my Beethoven was so bad, I needed to learn a new sonata and come back next year.

Since I did not want to be a solo piano performer, and as a teacher, I wasn't interested in grooming performers, and since the jury preparation had been so unpleasant, I lost all desire to finish the process. I would certainly not make myself learn a new sonata. But now I had no music degree and no letters after my name; only a growing belief in myself. Before long, I stopped worrying about it. When asked if my degree was in music, I said,

"Nope. I'm one sonata short of certification."

The Revenge Aria

I FOUND A NEW VOICE TEACHER, Marge Sackett. She took one look at me, all jacked up, my ribs sticking out from Tacoma to Everett as I had been taught, and suggested that I slouch a little.

She also said, "I have never said this to a student before, but do you think you could sing with a less open throat?"

Marge took apart my whole technique. I learned to sing with a more relaxed soft palate and less contrivance. The breath found more places to resonate. It was an easier way to sing and Marge was much more fun to work with. The new technique meant I didn't get as vocally tired, but I still hadn't enough vocal stamina to do, say, an opera or a Broadway show.

Marge used an accompanist at her lessons. Steve was the music director at a church in north Seattle. After playing for my lessons for a year, he asked me if I was interested in coming aboard as the paid soprano soloist at his church. I would sing every Sunday with the choir but I could also solo as often as I had something ready to sing.

The music part of it worked out beautifully. I loved working with Steve. He was an immensely talented musician without the usual overwrought ego. An unflappable director, he played the organ in his stocking feet and directed the choir with his head, his elbow, his shoulder, and whatever hand he could occasionally spare. He had no end of patience with the choir. Though it was a musical bunch, its primary goal was to enjoy itself;

that in itself is a great spiritual secret that eludes a lot of musicians. He told me that his job at the church was recreation for him. His enjoyment was infectious. I sang every Sunday for six years. Steve was the main reason I lasted as long as I did.

I sang solos: the *Benedictus* from Haydn's *Small Organ Mass,* every soprano solo from *Messiah*, and every scrap of churchy music by Handel I could find. Steve accompanied me on the organ or the piano. Several times a year, he'd bring in a small orchestra; singing with them was always a thrill. I sang the soprano solos in Schubert's Mass in G when I had laryngitis. I couldn't talk, but somehow I could sing.

There were moments of wonder and of grace in some of those performances. There was an intimacy in making music with Steve. He seemed to know intuitively what I wanted or was going to do. The intensity felt electric at times, like more energy than was possible got distilled into the measures of the music. Measures that then were gone forever. I often thought that the great thing was to live through the experience of the music, then continue to live, and not be reaching back, trying to recapture what would never again be.

In addition to being the soprano soloist, I became the substitute organist. In this I was lucky: even in contrast to Steve, I don't think the church realized how badly I played. I had a smattering of technique: I could move up and down the keyboard connecting thirds or sixths and I could crawl around enough to keep the sound constant. I quickly learned that if I pulled out the 16 foot stops, I could simulate the pedals without actually playing them. I practiced on my own time but did not pedal for public consumption. The church's forbearance allowed my organ playing to improve.

One Sunday afternoon, the choir did a Broadway revue in the sanctuary after the regular morning service. I invited Doug and was stunned when he told me he wouldn't come. I was seeing him twice a week by now because that helped control the panic attacks. But it also encouraged me to fantasize that I was more than his client, just like I had been more than my father's daughter.

"I won't come to your concert," he said. "Because it's outside the boundaries of our relationship."

I hated it when he talked like that. "You mean those Fucking Boundaries?" I demanded, unaware of any irony.

The day of the Broadway show was a case study in boundary violations.

I had invited my parents before I learned my father would be out of town. Since I didn't think fast enough to tell my mother the program had been canceled, I told her to come no earlier than 1:30. I had a lot of numbers and I didn't want her hanging around making demands of me before I had to sing.

I was sitting in the choir loft with the rest of the choir, watching the church fill up when, at 9:55 AM, my mother wandered in. She came halfway down the aisle, sat in a pew, got up, backed into the aisle, turned in a complete circle, and began wobbling toward the door. An usher intercepted her and helped her sit down

I watch in horrified fascination. "She has finally lost it," I thought. "She has lost her mind completely and she had to come here to do it."

I tried to forget she was there during the service. After the benediction, she stood up and looked around uncertainly. I walked out with the choir, and reminded myself to breathe. My mother was such a loose cannon, I never knew what she was going to do that would either humiliate me, or require all my energy to undo. I always tried to avoid contact with her before I had to sing, but it was a small, uncomplicated church and she found me on the stairs.

"Oh, Elena," she was giggling and seemed proud of something. "I locked my keys in the car! Help me get it open."

"I asked you not to come until this afternoon."

"Oh, don't be that way. Come on."

"No," I snapped. I was so uncomfortable with the word, I needed to work up a certain amount of indignation to get it out. "You are on your own. Don't come around me until after the show."

As I went into the social hall, I saw a strange man being escorted out of the boiler room by a church elder, rather like an arrest. Things were getting curiouser and curiouser. I filled a plate at the potluck and retired to a protected corner of the choir room to eat. Before long the tenor soloist joined me. He looked pained.

"My stepfather is here. He likes to wander."

"Was that him in the boiler room a bit ago?"

"Probably. Now he's out helping some lady who locked her keys in her car."

We ate in silent commiseration.

The Broadway Revue was a success but the real show—for me—had been my mother. By the end of the afternoon, I was angry and tired and my mother was hurt. She left after telling me how ungrateful I was.

I sang two solo recitals in that church with Steve as my impeccable accompanist. For the first recital, I sang *Jauchzet Gott in allen Landen*, the Bach cantata for soprano; a set of songs by John Duke and selections from *Brigadoon*.

I had asked my mother to not come looking for me before the recital, but half an hour before show time she appeared in the choir room where Marge was helping me warm up. She had managed to remember that I didn't want to talk to her so she addressed everything to Marge.

"Don't you think she has too much makeup on?" she began.

Marge said smoothly, "I think she could use a little more actually. It's performance makeup, you know."

My mother squeezed her hands, "I just hope she shows some confidence this time." With that she left the room.

There was a long silence. Then Marge said, "Hmm, I see what you mean."

My parents had brought Lillian, the woman who had hosted my first recital In Olympia. My mother had always energetically tried to make me be friends with her friends.

"You should visit Lillian. She asks about you. You know you sang your first recital in her house."

"I am not spending the rest of my life being grateful to Lillian that she let me sing a recital in her house."

Lillian was there as my parents' guests. In the reception following my recital, people lined up to congratulate me as though I was a bride. My mother infiltrated the line, encouraging people—ordering them, actually— to get something to eat first: They could talk to me later, the line was too long, she had made spanokopita and it was getting cold. When she had succeeded in peeling off half the line, she sidled up to me and remonstrated in a low voice, "Did you speak to Lillian?"

I shook her off in irritation. "Leave me alone."

She touched my cheek. "Is that a pimple?" she asked.

"Oh look," I said. "Is that a piece of your spanakopita on the floor." I moved to the other end of the line.

Lester would not have approved of the announcement flyers for my second recital. I billed myself as singing "Death-defying operatic arias, bucolic English songs, and bird imitations." I sang Schubert's *Der Hirt auf dem Felsen*, with a friend playing the clarinet part. I sang "Lo, Hear the Gentle Lark," "The Silver Song" from The *Ballad of Baby Doe,* and Bernstein's *I Hate Music.*

I sang The Queen of the Night's "Der Holle Racht" from *The Magic Flute*. Lester had once told me that I would never be able to sing the Queen of the Night's revenge aria because I lacked the temperament. He said there would be a personality conflict. As it happened, I did quite well singing the rageful mother. Steve used to say I could sing the Queen of the Night for breakfast.

Elena's Lament

I DIDN'T LIKE THE CHURCH SERVICES but I wanted the singing experience, and I liked the attention and the money. But I found it almost unbearable to sit through the sermons.

During a sermon about the sacrificing servant, the minister described a revelation he had had about his own selfishness. He detailed the sacrifices he was making in his daily comforts in order to serve others. I waited for a punch line that never came. His sacrifices were so bush league I wanted to laugh. Even Christians might not think it reasonable for a sacrificial servant to give up the amount of self I had jettisoned in my life. Suddenly I didn't want to laugh. I couldn't sit still. I was panicking. I left the service to get some breathing room.

I found ways of not letting the service influence me. I thought about my paycheck. I gazed at the stained glass rose window in back of the sanctuary and zoned out. During the sermons, I worked my way slowly through the hymnal, making note of any line that still had meaning for me:

Yet in thy dark streets shineth the everlasting light.

—

Awake, my soul, and sing!

—

Through many dangers, toils, and snares I have already come;
'Tis grace has brought me safe thus far and grace will lead me home.

———

The words were threads that reached back to my childhood. I pulled them through time to where I sat in the choir loft, holding the pieces of myself together. There was something in those old hymns I didn't want to lose; the melodies, the stability of the harmonies, and the fragments of texts that didn't need to involve the Christian God so much as my own sturdy spirit. I would carry those threads with me and weave them into new patterns. Eventually I would find dwellings where I felt more at home than I did in a church.

But in the meantime, I wrote a letter to the church staff. One of my critical, mince-no-words letters such as I had written to various doctors. I included information about my depression and panic attacks and how I was finding nothing, *nothing* in Christianity that was doing anything, *anything* except causing more pain. I was starkly honest and at the same time, gave them information they could use to make their church more vital and meaningful to real people. It was a win-win situation, I thought.

I heard nothing from anyone for two months. Then the minister called me to say he had been very concerned about my depression.

"It's been two months," I said. "I could have killed myself in that time."

I got a call from a church elder. He wanted to meet with me but wouldn't say why. It was very cloak and dagger. I asked Steve if he knew anything about it.

He said, "It's about that letter you wrote."

"Great," I thought. "They want to talk about my suggestions for making the church more relevant."

Juliet went with me. But the interview was not about the church's shortcomings. It was about my own. The Elder brought out a list he had compiled from his own observations:

Once I did not participate in communion. Check.

Once I had walked out during a sermon. Check.

Once my eyes were open during prayer.

You're kidding?

No.

Check

The list went on. I was paid staff. They could not have paid staff who were not on a spiritual path.

Juliet defended me. "Just because Elena is not benefiting from what this church teaches does not mean she is not on a spiritual path," she said.

The Elder was impassive. Either all these behaviors had to change or I would have to leave my position.

I left my position.

That afternoon, I went home and got out my New American Standard Bible, the Bible I had been using since high school, the only Christian book left in the house. I had long since tossed out all the Christian self-help books with titles like *Your Half of the Apple*, *My Utmost for His Highest*, *A Long Obedience in the Same Direction*, and *Where is God When It Hurts*, *Hinds Feet on High Places*, a truly appalling book. Actually they are all appalling. I got rid of all the C.S Lewis in a later sweep.

But I still had the Bible. An educated person keeps a Bible in the house. For reference, in case something comes up in Shakespeare she needs to look up. It wasn't because I was a Christian and believed this stuff. In truth, I was afraid to get rid of a Bible. I grew up in a household where a Bible was sacred, holy. We were not allowed to put anything on top of a Bible. Not a piece of paper, a Kleenex, or God forbid, a coffee cup.

I put on a recording of Janet Baker singing "Dido's Lament" from Purcell's *Dido and Aeneas* and cranked it up loud. I sat on the floor and tore the leather cover off the Bible. This took some doing and I was panting when it came off.

I yanked out hunks of pages, full of penciled margin notes. Genesis, Exodus.

"When I am laid, am laid in earth," Janet Baker's luscious voice filled the room.

The Psalms and the Prophets came out. My body shook.

"May my wrongs create no trouble, no trouble in thy breast."

I ripped out the gospels and threw them on the growing pile.

"Remember me, but ah, forget my fate!"

I ripped out the Epistles and Revelation, threw myself on the mound, and sobbed.

"Remember me, but, ah, forget my fate."

It was positively operatic. When I got up, I felt spacious on the inside. Tired, but spacious.

Creating Trouble

I stuffed the ripped Bible into a garbage bag, took it into therapy and upended it on the floor of the consulting room. Doug raised an eyebrow. He was used to my grand gestures; even so there was an almost imperceptible smile on his face.

"That looks like a Bible," he commented.

By this time, Doug was in a new office with a higher fee and was driving a teal Mazda pickup that I had paid for. He was wearing suits and ties. The braces were off his teeth. His hair had almost completely disappeared and he had a beard and mustache. I had been seeing him for eight years. I still called several times a week when I got panicky.

When I first started telephoning Doug, I remembered how problematic it had become for me when Lester gave me free lessons. I asked him if he wanted me to pay for the phone calls. I saw him start to shake his head. From the almost "No" of his head to the "OK, what do you want to pay?" that came out of his mouth, I was to be out thousands and thousands of more dollars in the years to come. And I would fight him Every. Penny. Of. The. Way.

I called him a lot. I knew no other way to cope. I called so often, he finally told me he didn't want me to call him at home.

"You can leave a message on my machine. I check it several times a day and I will call you back."

I was insulted. Calling him at home allowed me to have a private fantasy that I was part of his family, something I desperately wished I was.

"Don't you even have a pager? Other people have therapists who are *on call* 24 hours a day," I complained.

"I know that," he said. "It's a reasonable thing to expect from a parent when you're a child, but not between one adult and another."

"But isn't therapy re-parenting?" I had read this somewhere.

So had Doug. "No," he said.

With that fantasy exposed, I tried something else. "Well, God, you're so cold! You're so fucking clinical! I feel like a specimen."

I raged at him. I swore at him. I told him I hated him. He wasn't my parent but I screamed everything at him that I could not scream at them. I expressed my fury at being relegated to his answering machine by leaving angry messages. Once I left four messages in the space of five minutes:

"I can't take your call right now but if you leave your name and number, I'll get back to you as soon as possible."

"I'm calling to say I despise you."

"Hello, you've reached the psychotherapy offices of—"

"I think your ties are stupid."

"Hello, you've—"

"You pronounce the word 'appreciate' like a hick. Not that you ever direct that word to me."

"Hello—"

"You don't really know what you're doing with me do you? You're not very competent."

When I got that bout of rage out of my system, I felt unbearably anxious. How could he not terminate me after that? I left a message that I needed to talk to him. He called me right back; calm and dispassionate.

"God," I said. "You're so Scandinavian!"

After the Kleenex box, I never threw anything else, but I talked about a recurring fantasy of throwing a cup of coffee on him. "If I splashed coffee all over you, what would you do?"

"I'd say, 'See you next session.'"

"But what if it was the beginning of the session?" I was slow on the uptake here. "When the coffee was good and hot."

He looked at me quizzically.

"Oh," I said feebly. "I guess that would be the end of the session."

"Damn straight."

When Doug was recovering from a herniated disc, walking with a cane, and was quite obviously in some discomfort, I told him I wanted to flip his "fucking little business cards" all over the room and leave him to pick them up. As I swept out the door that day, my coat accidentally knocked all the fucking little business cards on the floor. I was terrified that the next session would be my last. Instead we just talked. We found words.

My experience of transference was intense. I was a three year old. He was my parent. It was absolutely real to me. Often I was stunned that I had to leave after 50 minutes. Some therapists try to discourage transference or to acknowledge it without working with it. Doug needed my transference to do the kind of work he did best. I knew intuitively that it was the kind of work I wanted to do, too; but for there to be a useful transference—one that could lead to me having new experiences—there needed to be greater dependence. This terrified me. For years, the best I could do was to hang somewhere between dependence and trust. I was dependent but did not trust Doug enough to let the dependence help me.

I had fantasies of all kinds about Doug. Sexual, paternal, sadistic, friendly. I loved him. I hated him. But the man I carried around in my mind wasn't the man in the office. The man in my fantasies raised dahlias, listened to Mahler, and didn't clutter up my sessions with his judgments and moods. The man in the office was a jock and an oenophile who listened to Sinatra, and sometimes did clutter up my sessions with his stuff.

When face to face with him, I was quite often struck dumb because he was not the fantasy. It was slow going, sorting out the transference, the fantasy and what was a viable relationship between us.

"If someone propped me up in a chair and paid me $40, I could sit there and say 'You're feeling sad, you're feeling angry,'" I yelled

A flush of red spread down his face, top to bottom, followed immediately by impassivity, as though a window shade had been drawn to obscure the drama inside the house. I was fascinated. I had finally gotten to him.

I didn't know it at the time, but Doug himself was struggling with his own depression. Years later, he said, "I had the same repressive religious upbringing that you did. How could I not be depressed?"

"How did you cope with me?"

"You were a relief sometimes because I could forget myself."

Some of what went on in my therapy with Doug is just what goes on in therapy; it can be a huge mess that takes a long time to sort through; a trashed apartment with hidden forensic evidence. It's tricky in the early stages when the client needs to believe the therapist doesn't have any messes of his own. Doug and I sorted through the trash together; two human beings doing the best we could with the capacities we had. When are any of us more than this?

But that is a generosity I have now. I didn't think so benevolently when I felt ripped open in sessions. When I had to stuff myself back inside and hold together until the next time. I felt re-traumatized, but I was so dependent I couldn't leave. I couldn't leave until I had gotten the Thing that when I had it, I would know it. The Thing my parents were supposed to have given me. I thought I could eventually get it from Doug.

This was still an inchoate idea; I didn't quite *know* that this was what I thought. If I had been able to verbalize it, I might not have done what I did do: I found Doug's home address from a piece of mail sitting in his car. I went looking for his house. I felt so guilty it took me a couple of trips before I made it all the way there. I cruised by the house and tried to memorize it. It was a split level like the red house of my childhood, and there was wood piled up against one side. That's all I remember about the experience except for a short-lived calm feeling.

I couldn't wait to talk about it with Doug. When I told him I had found his house, I knew he would suddenly understand all the things I couldn't explain. In my next session, I prattled on for quite a while before I realized it was not going as planned.

He was furious. He was frightened. "Elena, if you drive by my house again, it will be the end of your therapy."

That session ended badly and so did a lot of sessions for a long time after that. Everything seemed to refer back to The Incident of my finding Doug's house. I had achieved a kind of specialness but not the kind I had envisioned and not one that felt good.

The Incident set me back quite a ways if I was ever going to get that birthright thing from Doug. His reaction had frightened me. Therapy deteriorated but I hung on. I thought he was withholding what I needed, but I was going to get it if I had to bite it off him. His fee for both sessions and phone calls went up every year. I still wasn't getting what

I needed, yet I couldn't leave. I felt exploited. I thought of him as my dealer.

At the same time, I tried to protect myself from the process I was paying him for. "All I want is to get through this hour and get out of here without you helping me," I said more than once. It was exhausting. It was like trying to run underwater.

Juliet had taken my suggestion that she consult with Doug and she liked him enough to start therapy. For a while this was fun for us. We talked about him and speculated about his life. When a session had been especially hard, it was a relief to go over it with Juliet.

But before long, we had a play within a play: I took the role of Juliet's older sister, in competition with her for parental love and approval. Juliet was sure Doug loved me more because I had been there first.

Juliet played the part of my mother, the person I had taken my father/ Arthur away from. I privately agreed that I was special to Doug because it made me temporarily forget what an awful time I was having with him.

Doug sat in his office and, on cue, repeated his therapist lines:

"So in the dream, what part of you is the didgeridoo player?"

"So, you're angry."

"Our time is up now. We need to stop."

I did not wear bras in those days. Juliet asked me, "Do your nipples show like that when you are with Doug?" The look in her eyes was unreadable.

She sounded like my mother. It was critical that I continue to think of myself as a sexless block of wood. I couldn't afford to understand what might be going on under the surface. The friendship with Juliet began to feel as precarious as the relationship with Doug.

I was doing no better at home than I was in therapy. If the neighbors in my previous home had been a bad dream, I was about to have a pro-longed nightmare. A year after buying my house, an indeterminate number of people moved next door. There were never less than seven vehicles in their driveway, spilling into the street and running at odd angles over our property lines. Men and women came and went at all hours of the day and night, talking, or more often yelling at each other, gunning their car engines, and blasting their stereos.

Though at first it was difficult to tell who actually lived there, I soon became privy to more information than I wanted. When I was in my back yard, watering my blueberry bushes, I learned the names of the regulars. I heard when they got their periods and when the semen on the bed sheets was getting too funky and a load of laundry was required. I learned that Monica wanted a baby but not a husband so she was interviewing men for stud purposes. Her radar was out for what she considered "good blood." In due time she became pregnant and I heard all about that. Everything these women did, they did at full volume.

I said hello every now and again, trying to find a place where there might be some generosity of feeling to mediate their unpredictable noise. I was terrified of them. My anxiety was so high I stopped making distinctions about when it became an actual panic episode. I lived in a near constant feeling of liquidating.

They acquired a dog with a hoarse, high-pitched bark. Fiko could bark eight hours at a stretch; I know because once I clocked it. One night I heard a series of shrieking, piercing squeals and my first thought—hope, really—was that Fiko had gotten entangled in a rope and was hanging himself. Instead it turned out to be a new puppy that soon learned how to get through the fence and poop in my yard. They got rid of the puppy. Fiko barked on.

I tried making friends with Fiko. I fed him pounds of dog biscuits and commiserated with him over the experience of being ignored. He slobbered all over me and kept right on barking. My mind hooked up an impression of neglect with the sound of a dog barking. Now I had a second trigger for panic attacks.

I tried talking to the neighbors. I called their landlord. I tried to enlist the help of other neighbors and in doing so, found out that the people living to the north and south of who I now thought of as Those Fucking Neighbors, were deaf. I tracked down every city official and agency I could find to enlist their help. I had a whole file on noise ordinances, but no solutions. I called the police on a regular basis, also with no lasting result except to annoy the police. I applied to mediation through the city, but the neighbors refused to cooperate. Their exact words to the mediator were, "Fuck off."

Solar Eclipse

I WANTED TO RUN AWAY AND START OVER. I called my Cornish cousins and got an enthusiastic invitation to come for Christmas. I packed up and left, excited and happy to be getting away. But as soon as I walked off the plane at Heathrow, I started panicking and I didn't know why. Because I didn't know why, I didn't say anything. I tried to beat it back. It was like trying to beat back the surf with a toothpick. I was met by Joy and Wendy, Hazel's great nieces. The three of us drove the five hours to Cornwall. I held myself together in the car and pretended to sleep.

I hadn't called Doug at his home number in years but I still knew it by heart. I called him from Cornwall on Christmas Day. That was how I learned the news that he was divorced and no longer living in the house I had located, and where I still pictured him living. I couldn't have anticipated how much I needed a secure sense of Doug being happily married and living in the house I had seen. I loved him in the way I had loved Arthur but I needed to know that this man was out of reach because only then did he feel safe. This news, learned while I was far away from home, caused another room in my psychic house to flood. The feeling of liquefying came in waves, each time more forceful, as though with each crash of panic, I was determined to finally spill out onto the floor, once and for all.

Not for nothing had I spent 39 years building a fortress around my feelings. My facade participated in the holiday. That no one knew me all that well made it easier. Everyone was wonderful to me; lovely, as they say. I got my Cornish Christmas, complete with the crackers, paper hats, seven veg, and a Christmas cake on Boxing Day. I only wish I had been there to experience it.

We made a little run out to Looe on Boxing Day. There on the beach were hundreds of tiny cockles in the most amazing colors: soft yellow, orange and gold; blues, violets. Wendy helped me gather up handfuls of them. It was a cold rainy day, but the sun broke through as I stood up from the shell collecting, and a full rainbow stretched across the beach. It was a good omen, a promise that things would get better.

More immediately, however, my back went into a ferocious spasm. When I came home from Cornwall it was painful to move; and for a long time I didn't except to teach. I lay on the couch and thought, "I am 39 years old and I guess this is what the rest of my life will be: back pain and depression." I didn't get the help I needed because I didn't trust people who might help and I was ashamed that my body hurt at all. It somehow seemed to be proof that I was defective to start with. It hurt to breathe. I stopped singing.

One night, I put a plastic bag over my head and tied it tight. Then I started in on my wrists with a razor blade. That's as far as I got. I didn't think it would be so hard. I thought that just making the decision would be the hard thing. I felt nauseated and frightened. I stopped. I put down the blade and took the bag off my head.

I sat for a while. I felt a tiny flickering of something inside me, something quite lovely; a pilot light that was on long after I thought I had junked the stove. A tiny but sturdy flicker that conveyed this message: "You can't do this." Nothing particularly profound, but ramifications ensued: if killing myself wasn't an option, I had to find a different way to live.

I knew the pilot light was my Spirit. The name Elena means *Light*. What I found deep inside me was *my* light, *my* spirit; *Elena*, not Jesus. The distinction was important to me. It was important to know that I was precious, because I was Me, period. Being a reflection of Jesus was no different than being a reflection of my mother. In both cases, I had no substance. I only existed to reflect someone else. In the panic attacks, I had no substance: I was liquefying and spilling onto the floor. Christianity teaches that we exist for God and we are a reflection of Him. Something in this idea was at the root of my depression.

My life felt like a vacant lot in a bombed out neighborhood. For years I had toyed with the idea that the way out was suicide. The despair on that road is so heavy and incapacitating; it takes enormous amounts of energy to turn back. It's better to not go there at all. I needed to find my way through unfamiliar streets to houses with gardens and living people. But for now all I could manage was to sit by the side of the road in a weak patch of sun.

Frances Rides Again

"SHE SAID YOU SOUNDED LIKE A REAL JERK," I told Doug. He nodded gravely.

"OK, that was a joke," I said. A feeble little joke.

I had decided to leave therapy. I consulted with another therapist who concurred that Doug and I seemed to be struggling and that he was understandably defensive that I had discovered his house. *I* didn't find it understandable but we didn't get into that. She said that while much of the same stuff would come up in me no matter who I was seeing for therapy, I might have an easier time sorting through it with someone else.

I had gotten through the suicide episode with Doug being out of town and I deeply resented him for not being available. The relationship had become intolerable for both of us. My little pilot light was so weak, I had a sensation of being suffocated, assaulted by his personality. He sat across the room from me and hardly moved but it still felt like Andy yelling at me, like Lester criticizing my song interpretations, like my father sitting, drunk, on my bed; like my mother bursting into my bedroom. I felt squeezed out of myself, liquefying and running all over the floor. I was intensely attached to Doug. But I wanted him to be something I couldn't verbalize. Leaving therapy was like a romantic break-up. It felt like the end of the world. A week later the friendship with Juliet, which had been like a ship going down for some time, finally slipped into the sea. She and I had formed a sticky mess of envy, competition and projection that neither of us was equipped to talk about with the other. If Doug had involved himself, the friendship might have been salvaged, but that wasn't his job.

I had always found Juliet warm and sympathetic, something I needed so desperately in a friend that when I found it, I clutched at it. I was unable to see her except through a longing for love and warmth. I didn't recognize how resentful I felt when I was used in this same way by other people. It never occurred to me that Juliet might have found this repressive, that she might have resented me because I demanded so much for myself and recognized so little of her.

In a phone call, Juliet said that she hoped things went well for me in the rest of my life. She was oblique about it, she hated scenes. I was shocked. I hadn't seen it coming because I was so overwhelmed with myself. It was years before I could appreciate how overwhelming I might have been to Juliet.

I told my parents about my suicide attempt. They didn't say much. A few weeks later, I got a phone call from my father, who said rather coldly that he and my mother had talked about it and had come to the conclusion that there wasn't anything they could do. For some reason, I was shocked. I was used to their tone-deafness, but this still amazed me. And hurt. It seemed like one or the other of them could at least have managed to say they were glad I was still alive.

It seemed to me that they might feel some curiosity about what was going on with me and because they *loved* me, they might be willing to look at how they *may* have contributed to my difficulties in life. But that would have required some self-reflection and these were people who did not Dwell on the Past. My mother's diagnoses were either I was not Right With God or I wasn't eating enough broccoli. My father always pleaded parental ignorance by virtue of having been an orphan.

Alternately, I thought they were withholding something they would give me if they just understood how desperately I wanted to feel loved and understood. The suicide attempt might squeeze out of them what nothing else had. The suicide attempt was my trump card. I had played it and lost a therapist, my best friend, and my parents.

It was the blackest time of my life. In the mornings, I woke up sobbing and spent the day in and out of tears. I walked around in the world, went into the post office and grocery store, but I felt like I was sliced down the front and my insides were hanging out and trailing behind me. I didn't understand why no one noticed and asked if they could help.

One good thing I did, because I could think of nothing else to do, was to make lists of goodness. Things like "the sky is blue today" or "that apple tasted good." Homely, small things. The world felt very small, like a little hole. I sat in the little hole and made my lists.

My students kept coming. It was a relief to work. It gave me some space from the difficult feelings. And I realized that in spite of all the drama behind the scenes, I was a good teacher. I was learning and growing and paying attention. I had some worth.

A psychiatrist added Lithium to the Prozac and Xanax I was already taking. Over medicated, I stumbled when I walked. I thought I couldn't function without drugs and this, in turn, prevented me from finding alternate ways through my difficulties. When I complained to the psychiatrist, he became exasperated,

"But you are doing so much better!"

"*My God*, in whose world?" I was alarmed. Either he hadn't been listening to me or I had unaccountably stopped speaking English.

This drug regimen was for someone else. Years later, if I took a quarter of a milligram of Xanax to help me sleep at night, I would be groggy until mid-afternoon the next day. But during this period, I was taking 5 mg before noon and was still having panic attacks.

I took myself off the Prozac gradually and hoarded the Xanax for my worst episodes. More immediately, I dumped the Lithium down the toilet and packed myself off to Buncombe Creek to see my Aunt Frances.

Frances had lost quite a bit of her magic during the drunken summer I spent with them. But when I walked off the plane at the Dallas airport and saw her, fifteen years of silently missing her exploded inside me.

My uncle Don had died. Frances had been taking Prozac herself since his death so my recent foray into psychotropic drugs didn't faze her. But when I told her I had been suicidal, she pulled off the road.

"Why didn't you call me?" she asked.

I started to cry. "I had forgotten about you," I said.

Then, surprisingly, Frances said, "I knew there would be problems what with your daddy doin' you the way he did and usin' you for his own ends. And your mother wasn't any help; she didn't understand. You been tryin' to grow up for a long time and you haven't had any help."

Later that night, after a supper of fried catfish and hush puppies, Frances said, "You know, Lainie, you're very smart. But you can be real dumb, too, about some things. You're innocent. You know about some of the ugliness in the world, but you have an innocence that protects you. If you didn't have that, you'd have never made it through some of things that have happened to you and some of the things you've seen. It's one of the loveliest things about you. Your therapist must surely have told you that."

I grinned, "Not exactly," I said.

She nodded. "Well, no, he couldn't be that blunt."

We went into Madill the next day for lunch. I saw a little chain in a gift shop that I wanted to buy but Frances said to wait, she had something to show me. Back home she hauled out all her jewelry: piles of silver and gold chains, rings and bracelets of topaz, emeralds, diamonds, amethyst, garnet, zircon, and her favorite, peridot. She told me to take whatever I wanted and that the silver would look best with my coloring.

I knew where most of her stash had come from. Don had given her some jewelry, but since his death, Frances had QVC going all day long. She liked the jewelry shows best so when they came on she would sit and watch with a pen and notebook. I loved watching TV with Frances. Like my mother, she kept up a running commentary, but unlike my mother, Frances made me laugh.

She knew all the gossip about the QVC hosts. "Now this young man here, he's engaged to that little mouse that was on last hour. It's not gonna work out. They aren't right for each other. Now he and that Diamonique host, they were good friends but they had a falling out. I think they've made up. The blonde next hour, she is always getting sick and needing to make up her hours so she subs for the mouse."

Since the hosts rarely came on together and this was well before the Internet, I don't know where Frances sniffed out her information. But her commentary was more interesting than the QVC hosts. She never worried about whether anyone was wearing underpants. She was more likely to say something like, "Now there's a nice cleavage. Lainie, we ought to find you a good bustier like that one's wearing. You have such pretty breasts."

From her pile of jewelry Frances gave me two silver herringbone chains and a bracelet, several diamond cut figure eight silver chains, and a gold Gucci bracelet. She wanted me to have 10 cocktail rings, one for each finger and thumb—for when I played the piano—but I said I didn't fancy myself as Liberace. Instead I picked out a ring set with an opal and two rubies and another with a row of Montana jade.

"Now," she said, "Do you still want that grubby little chain?"

We laughed. Frances got out the silver polish and cleaning solutions and I spent the afternoon playing with her jewelry. I cleaned it, and then put it on until I was wearing everything just like I had when I was six years old.

Launching Forth Filaments

BACK IN SEATTLE, I HAD SCRAPS OF MY LIFE to pick up. After the suicide attempt, after terminating with Doug, after the shock of losing Juliet, and after I had exhausted all but criminal means of coping with Those Fucking Neighbors, I did go away and start over. I bought a townhouse on the edge of a greenbelt in Bothell, 25 minutes northeast of Seattle. I moved my music studio into the Phinney Neighborhood Center, in proximity to most of my students who all seem to live within half a mile of each other in the Ballard neighborhood of Seattle.

I went to see a counselor who was different from Doug in every conceivable way. She was female, had a big smear of new age ideas, and worked from a lot of different traditions. I was game to try anything: past life regression, hypnotherapy, crystals, art, writing, Shen, craniosacral. It was good to talk to a woman and everything helped a little. But she worked out of her home, she talked more about herself than I wanted to hear, and her ideas were simplistic.

She seemed almost disgusted that I would spend so much of my time being depressed. She told me I needed to relegate the time I spent in depression to a few hours at most and to spend the rest of my time in creative endeavors.

"It's not good for your mental health to be so depressed," she told me.

My physical health followed my emotional health. I developed tinnitus. It drove me crazy for a while. Actually I thought the tinnitus was proof I was already crazy. I spent the next 10 years in a fruitless search for a cure. I went on a rotation diet for two years; this didn't help the tinnitus but I lost some weight and learned what star fruit and amaranth were. Cranio-sacral technique helped with anxiety but not with the ear ringing. In the end, learning to live with the tinnitus was what made its intensity recede.

That same year, I began to have pain from sciatica and degenerated discs. I stopped seeing doctors altogether. For years, I went to an acupuncture and Oriental medicine clinic for everything medical. I went through chiropractors, massage therapists and physical therapists like water. I did two years of Movement Therapy concurrent with two years of myo-fascial release therapy. I tried yoga, Aston patterning, Feldenkrais, Tai Chi, and two courses of Hellerwork. Everything chipped away at both the physical and the emotional pain but there were no great leaps of relief.

In movement therapy, I discovered a mechanism that began to suck the energy out of the panic attacks. I crawled into a closet and closed the door. I sat in the dark and ran my hands up and down my body, telling myself, "Here you are. This is you. You aren't spilling out anywhere." I did this until the panic coalesced into a huge ball in my throat, then I sobbed until it dispersed itself. I did this for months with lessening frequency until I could do a quickie version of it while waiting for a red light. I was far from being free of the panics, but the exercise helped enormously with making things more manageable.

I still got up early for what used to be my Bible Reading time. Now I read Joseph Campbell and Jean Shinoda Bolen. I started messing around with astrology as a mental exercise, like crossword puzzles, but then because I became fascinated with it and felt pulled into its world of symbols. I worked my way through Demetra George's beginning astrology book. I learned to do Tarot Cards, hooking them into what I was learning about astrological symbols and archetypes. I looked into Wiccan through Starhawk's writing. I started doing little rituals on the new and full moons and began paying attention to the seasons, to the cross-quarter days and to pagan holidays.

I learned Shamanic journeying and went on regular little meditative canoe trips. I put on a drumming CD and zoned out. I had never been able to meditate. The quiet was too reminiscent of my mother lying beside me in bed, repeating her mantra of "Go to sleep, toes; relax, toes," while I lay rigid as a board afraid that I wouldn't be able to relax. But the constant drum beat had a predictable reassurance. It lulled me into a place where I let go of my vigilance and let my imagination soothe me. I would get out of my figurative canoe feeling loved.

I may have been exploring new ideas but I was still struggling to extricate myself from fundamentalist thinking. I had a road map in my head, a mappa of my mundi, a template through which I squished all my experience. Astrology and Tarot cards lend themselves to fatalistic thinking. If one is already inclined that way, paganism can be just as tight a prison as any other belief system.

But when we first try to find our way out of traditions that haven't served us, we initially only plow our old worldview into a new field. We might be trying to plant new seeds, but we essentially grow the same crop. It takes a long time and a lot of help for new growth to take root in new earth.

Everything helped a little. I let ideas trickle into me, filling receptive crevices and holes. Whatever engaged my imagination and intuitive nature stayed with me. Following a tradition just because it was A Tradition had not served me well in life. I would rather have stuck pins in myself.

Have Yourself a Merry Little Christmas

I HAD RUN AWAY TO ENGLAND FOR ONE CHRISTMAS, and I had moved out of the city, but I was still keeping up pretensions with my family. My brother had moved to Seattle and was making his living as a potter. I went to his sales and bought his pots. I had them all over my house and I gave them as gifts. But he showed no interest in my life. He had never heard me sing. I understood his beef with our parents but I didn't understand why he lumped me with them. We had both grown up in the same environment, victims of the same forces. It was years before I had an inkling of how our upbringing had affected him.

A week before one Christmas a foot of snow fell, then immediately froze, well before Seattle's three snow plows could be found, rusting in the back of some city storage barn.

My mother called, "Alexander can't get out of his driveway. He told us it's too dangerous to drive so we aren't coming for Christmas."

"Mom, I was driving in the north end last night. The main streets are okay. The freeway is completely bare. You'll be fine."

"Oh, no. Alexander can't get out of his driveway. He said not to come so we aren't."

"Did you hear what *I* said?"

"We'll get together later for a family Christmas."

Two days later, my mother called again. "Alexander got out of his driveway. He says the main streets are okay and the freeway is completely bare. We're coming after all."

So I already felt marginalized when I set out to what would be my last family Christmas. It was a large gathering, hosted by folks my parents had kept up with since the Bellevue days. One guest was a doctor who was on call over the holiday. In the middle of dinner he took a call, came back to the table and announced to everyone: a woman who was depressed had just eaten an entire box of chocolates and now she wanted to kill herself. There were some laughs, some embarrassment, some expressions of disgust, and of sympathy.

I broke into a sweat. The dishes on the table started swimming and nausea welled up inside me. The woman could have been me. I pushed back from the table and excused myself. I couldn't get away fast enough. I have regrets about various outbursts of indignation I have indulged in. However I regret *not* having told this particular member of the medical profession to shut the fuck up.

I never shared another Christmas with my family. Bereft of my own, I became part of my Chinese friend Mai's extended family whose arms had been open to me for years had I only been able to see them. Mai was now married and had a child.

During her first two years in America, when she lived with me, Mai spent long hours sitting in an arm chair watching the activity on the street, eating hard candy and gaining weight. Fifteen years later, she again looked like the tiny girl who walked off the airplane in her Chinese pajamas, except now she was quite stylish with short slim skirts, spike heels, and gold jewelry. Her forehead was always slightly bunched, giving her a quizzical expression that gave way ten seconds after I said something that made her laugh. Her English was improved but it still took her a while to unravel a joke.

She had sponsored the immigration of a sister and several brothers who were all married and starting families. I was welcomed as the matriarch. I showed them how to have a bloated American Christmas and we carried on for many years while the family grew larger. Finally we exhausted ourselves, very nearly suffocated the lot of us in the Christmas wrapping paper. We settled down to a tradition of only a dinner at Christmas, and Dim Sum and gambling at Chinese New Year.

My own family had long ago dispensed with any kind of festive wrapping. We were like four hillbillies, each defending his plot of land with a shotgun. Any move toward another was met with suspicion, not with welcome. Once, in an effort to comply with my mother's demands that I call her, I did call to say hello.

"What do you want now?" she whined.

Finally I stopped talking to all of them. For nearly three years I didn't have any contact with my family. The panic attacks got fewer and farther between and the depression continued to stop just this side of being suicidal. I was living on the edge of a greenbelt. And I was almost out of the woods.

The OK Chorale

MAI'S FAMILY FOUND ME but I unexpectedly created another family for myself when I started a class for the University of Washington's Experimental College called "Part Singing." Not the catchiest of titles. Not the most elucidating either.

"Does it mean people sing only part of the time?"

"Does everyone sing in the same register?"

"Hey, can you teach me to yodel?"

The class was a modest success from the start but when I changed the name to The OK Chorale five years later, attendance doubled. The same people began coming back quarter after quarter. I had a community choir, not a class.

I started the Chorale in part because I wanted to hear voices singing in harmony and I wanted to improve my alto and learn to sing tenor and bass. I also wanted to sing different kinds of music than I generally heard with choirs. There were plenty of church choirs in Seattle with their limited repertoire, and plenty of big auditioned choirs that sang magnificent choral works and wrung the life out of its singers during the performance week. But where could someone go to sing "April is in my Mistress Face" and "Zombie Jamboree" all in the same quarter? I set out to create a choir that I wanted to be part of.

I played piano in rehearsals and learned to direct with a hand, an elbow, or nods of the head, just as Steve had done with the church choir I had left behind. I had no training in conducting but I developed my own style. I learned to sing alto, tenor and bass.

Quarters started to feel like sessions of summer camp. A lively, noisy group assembled, excited to see each other after a month's break. We rehearsed for two months, and then took our show on the road. We sang at the Northwest Folk Life Festival in May; at the Green Lake Luminarias and on the Christmas Ship in December; at Farmer's Markets, on the Puget Sound ferries, at bookstores and retirement homes.

A lot of singers came to their first rehearsal with some species of this story to tell me:

"The nuns told me to mouth the words."

"My father said I sounded like a chicken."

"My third grade teacher told me I couldn't sing in the pageant."

People with choir experience sometimes approached me with their tutorials. They asked if I was going add dynamics. They pointed out that the sopranos were holding their half notes for three counts. I took their lists and said thank you, but in the beginning I was intimidated. Nearly everyone, myself included, had the idea that music was about rehearsing something to perfection and having one chance to get it right in the performance.

But I also had the experience of working under Steve, the unflappable. I remembered how things came together when people were relaxed and enjoying themselves. I learned there had to be negotiables when working with real people with varying degrees of skill and experience. I was one of those real people. I had limitations. I didn't have to know everything. I was amazed at the cheerfulness with which the group accepted that.

In rehearsals I was swamped with all there was to cope with: the separate parts, putting the parts together, where to breathe, the phrasing, helping the non-music readers to catch up with the readers, encouraging others to not turn the pages of the music like they were reading the Sunday paper, thus dragging down the tempo.

Sometimes there was an eruption of differing opinions over where unintended dissonance was coming from. I had a rule: No accusing anyone else of being wrong. I didn't want my singers to be afraid of making mistakes. When the whole group was singing it was an aural hall of mirrors. I walked around during the singing and heard the sound change from every different square foot of the room. No one heard anything in a way that could be called absolute. It was positively psycho-analytic.

I needed music that required little in piano accompaniment and none of the bells and whistles that go with so much choir music. I arranged songs: Beatle songs, Broadway show tunes, folk and popular music. I picked songs I liked and tailored the arrangements for the voices in the Chorale. I had learned a little about choral arranging at Whitman and in my classes with Ken Benshoof. Over the years I worked on the arrangements so they had smoother voice leading and incorporated changes that had worked differently in reality than in my conceptions. I rewrote them so they were easier to read.

I didn't have a sound in my head that I expected The OK Chorale to fulfill. I wanted us to play together with what we had. I liked to try different things and see what worked. The Chorale was the test group for my arrangements. I matched the music to them not the other way around.

I wanted people to enjoy making music. I had an unshakable belief that this would make up for the disparity in voice quality and musicianship among the singers. I believed that when people weren't frightened of criticism, the sound would be free, open, and expressive. It worked. People in the Chorale enjoyed themselves and so did our audiences.

One of the tenors told me, "You know, the hours I spend here are the only ones in the week where I feel happy and relaxed and not worried about something."

I might have said much the same thing. The OK Chorale was a huge outward success but I was probably the last person to enjoy it. During rehearsals I was absorbed with the music and it gave me a break from myself. But I cried all the way to rehearsals and I cried all the way home. Depression is like that. It can ruin anything. It's a malevolent tyrant who has gained squatters' rights, who calls you home for dinner and then eats you from the inside out.

Hestia

S*OMETIMES WHILE IN THE COMPANY* of the malevolent tyrant, I had what I called "Hestia visitations." Hestia was the Greek goddess of home and hearth. I imagined her as the protector of my little pilot light. The visitations reminded me of the hypnogogic experiences I had as a child, the ones I learned later were called Krakower syndrome. As a child, when my terror felt annihilistic, my mind found a way to let me float in the womb until I went to sleep.

As an adult, I had a scorching contempt for myself. The Chorale was a fluke. Everyone would soon find out I didn't have a music degree, couldn't sing alto, hadn't taken a conducting class, no longer took voice lessons. I told myself that if I was worth anything, I wouldn't feel so empty and alone, and just in case that didn't sink in, I would add that I was fat. I was worthless and horrible because I was fat. Or I was fat because I was worthless and horrible. The logic went both ways. In the intensity of those flagellations a lovely, strong woman sometimes stepped into my imagination and put her arms around me. The vicious feelings temporarily subsided and I felt some relief.

The lovely strong woman took different forms. I sometimes encountered her in the world outside my mind: a mother called to ask if I would be willing to give her fourteen-year-old daughter singing lessons. The girl had been diagnosed with a terminal brain tumor. The mother had seen my name on a bulletin board at the Ronald MacDonald house where she and her daughter were staying. All traditional and experimental treatments had been exhausted, and the doctors had said to let her do whatever she wanted in these last few months. She wanted to sing.

My first impression was that Meagan looked about ten years old. She was slight and weak, half of her body propped up with a brace because it went in and out of paralysis. She had a delicate face with sad, tired eyes, and a sweet smile. Her head was swathed in a bright scarf. She wanted to sing a song that was popular at the time called "Hero." I played the introduction and out of Meagan's frail, skinny, dying body came a robust, pure voice singing that a hero lived inside her.

By the time she got to the end, I couldn't see the music for the tears in my eyes. The voice seemed to have no connection to the body which housed it. It had a life of its own, one that promised to go on generating life even after it left Meagan's body. Meagan herself seemed to have a sense of this. "I am going to surprise you all," she said.

I cried for days after my first lesson with Meagan. In all, I saw her about six times. We got together one last time at a recording studio in Pike Place Market called "Clatter and Din" where one of my adult students had arranged for Meagan to make a recording. Her left arm was now in a sling because it was starting to come out of its socket. She was on painkillers and had the flu. She, the Star, had brought me, the teacher, a bouquet of flowers. We put a headset on her, and her mother held her upright in the little glass booth. The studio staff brought her hot drinks, cold drinks, food, candy, anything she wanted. I hitched up to a keyboard in another room. I pushed a button to communicate with Meagan. We spent over an hour putting "Hero" on a tape.

I listened to the recording many times after Meagan died a week later. I would hear myself play the introduction and see Meagan through the glass, so tired her mother had to hold her head up for her. Then I'd hear her voice, strong and true; all the hope and vitality in the world coming through her little body.

She was my Hestia. Some kind of transaction took place between Meagan and me. I had felt so much despair in my life and had wanted to die for as long as I could remember. It seemed to me that Meagan was giving me a gift of her huge capacity for hope. She had more hope than she could contain by the time she met me. She was dying and didn't need Hope any longer; she had it to give away. I took it. I didn't know what it meant or how it would affect me, but I took it.

Frances Sails Away

MEAGAN'S DEATH WAS, IN FACT, A FORESHADOWING of a death closer to home. In January of my 40th year, I got a call from my flamboyant Aunt Frances. She had been diagnosed with pancreatic cancer and the doctors were giving her three months. There was a long pause while this news washed over me. I started to cry. I said, "I'm coming with you. I don't want to live in the world if you're not here."

"Oh, no, doll, you're staying here. But I want you to come visit me again before I get too far gone."

I flew to Texas City. I could see that Frances was dying, but her spirit was what it had always been; she seemed no different to me than when I was 13 and she was 40. Her eyes still sparkled in her wrinkled and jaundiced face, their radar roaming about for something to enjoy, to laugh at, to wink at, or to turn her wrath on. She still laughed that laugh: a giant wheeze that swept me up, wriggled me down and tickled me.

I stayed for a week. She might have been weak and in pain, but she was still present. She cooed over the phone to someone, throwing a pound of sugar at them, then hung up, muttering, "God damned heifer. Her and her dirty dog ways. Says she's swamped. I'll swamp her ass . . . what you need, sugar baby? You all want some ice tea? Hep yourself, darlin'. . . . and open that box of chocolates."

My second night Frances and I had the worst fight we'd ever had. Actually, I don't think we had ever fought, full stop. She had inexplicably made the suggestion that if I had had children of my own, I wouldn't have had the luxury of being as depressed as I'd always been. It sounded so much like my mother, I fought back as though Frances *was* my mother. I became hysterical and finally locked myself in my room. Frances, weak and doped up, slipped one of her sedatives under my door and went to bed.

I lay simmering most of the night, in spite of the sedative. In the morning, memory of the night before jolted me awake and I crept into Frances' room. "I was sure I had killed you," I said.

She laughed, "Hell, Lainie, I don't even remember what happened last night."

I didn't fill her in.

In addition to me almost killing her, Frances was contending with no appetite and was suffering from nausea. At the Krogers deli I asked for a spoonful of everything in the case. I wanted to find something Frances would eat. After a few days, I was having them create little meals for her.

"Everyone at the Krogers deli knows you're dying," I told her. Frances wheezed her wonderful laugh.

I wouldn't have known she was in pain if she hadn't kept mentioning it. She said she felt like all her organs were falling out. Here's Frances on hold for the doctor: "She'll probably tell me it's just the cancer. That or old age. Damned heifer, she spells my name with an 'i' instead of an 'e.' I keep telling her I have cancer, not a sex change."

Family members called every day and I heard my activities enumerated over the telephone: "Lainie took out the garbage twice and did laundry. Then she tootled all over town in Jerry and them's Bronco and walked the trail at City Hall Park. She brought in some ribs and stripped 'em off the bone into bitty pieces for me to eat. They gave her a card at the office so she could come and go at the gate and she made copies of some receipts I needed…"

The third night, Frances got out all the stuff she had set aside for me: more of her jewelry, a couple of outfits which I privately thought would be fun on Halloween, a mirror that had belonged to Aunt Ann, her muskrat-dyed mink fur coat, also great for Halloween; and a larger than life photograph of my uncle Don in his air force uniform. The photo was attached to a heavy board so it was a large, unwieldy portrait that was going to be a job getting home on the plane. She handed it to me reverently. It was the finest thing she could give me.

"I know you were crazy about your uncle Don," she said.

I thanked her, searching her face. There was no irony there. She believed it. The truth is that when I was small, I was terrified of my uncle Don. When I was older, I appreciated his Richmond sense of humor but beyond that, I thought he could be a big baby, and an ugly drunk. I wasn't crazy about him at all. Frances had always been the big attraction. But there was no need to say any of this now. After Don died, Frances was the first to concede that he had been no saint, but now that she was dying, she was entitled to whatever myth she chose to believe.

It was her daughter-in law, Ginny, who told me the full story. "She tried to give that photo to everyone in the family and no one wanted it. I'm afraid you're stuck with it, Lainie!"

The portrait was so big and heavy—not unlike Don himself—that it could have taken up a bus seat. Ginny and I hatched an idea whereby we could share the gift. I could keep him for now. When I got tired of him, I could package him up and ship him on a Greyhound to Texas. Ginny would send him to Yazoo City when the season changed and so on until everyone had a visit, then he'd come back to me and we'd start all over. We could all enjoy Don in a way we never had while he was alive. We never did it, of course; it would have been way too much trouble. But *that* is the Richmond sense of humor.

I came home from Texas feeling foggy and dull. My back and neck hurt. I woke myself up at night grinding my teeth. I fell back asleep into dreams and awoke, crying. I knew I would never see Frances again. I went up to St James Cathedral on Seattle's First Hill and lit a candle. When I said Frances' name, I started to sob and to ramble on about her dying. Grief had barged into my life like a big ship in a small harbor. I was helpless, watching all that it smashed through, all that it rearranged in my internal world.

The Taboo Triumvirate

IN RETROSPECT IT MADE SENSE TO ME that with Frances' impending death, I might go looking for someone who would never leave me, someone obsessed with me. Browsing one day in a new age book store in Seattle, a fellow browser struck up a conversation with me.

"What kinds of books are you looking for?" he asked me.

I noticed the load of books under his arm and said, "I was looking for astrology books but I see you have taken them all."

Thus began a four-month intensive with Marcus, a recent immigrant from West Africa who was married to an American. He told me he had seen my face in a dream and we were fated to be together. I found him physically attractive, he smelled delicious, and his skin was like warm chocolate. I was soon intoxicated with the feeling of being wanted.

I had come through the sexual revolution on a different path than pretty much everyone I knew. Most women with emotionally incestuous parents had had a series of sexual encounters and usually a couple of marriages by the time they hit 40; I hadn't even had sex with another person. In the Christian community this was considered right and proper. Every Christian woman who had sex "out of wedlock" regretted it. All my adult life I had gotten smarmy comments from Christians like: "God just hasn't brought that perfect person into your life yet because He has not finished perfecting you." This was a death sentence to someone who had been checking etiquette books out of the public library and embarking on self-improvement projects since she was eight years old. It made me stuff even more of myself into the little hole where I hid things I wanted to protect and usually only succeeded in losing.

Once I had asked my mother if she had ever enjoyed sex.

"God says that sex is good," she told me.

"But did you ever enjoy it?"

"Are you still plucking your eyebrows?"

I had pressed my parents for information that might help me. My mother said, "Your dad, he gets what he wants."

My father said, "Your mother is like a milkmaid." I interpreted this to mean he thought my mother was lusty.

And I think that was the last I cared to hear about their sex life.

Accepting the Christian smarminess conveniently cloaked how frightened I was. Until Marcus came along, I thought I was frightened of sex but that was soon dispelled. I loved sex. I was eager to try everything. With Marcus there was lots of activity, no judgments.

Marcus was separated from his American wife and told me he wanted a divorce from her. Since he needed to be married to an American in order to stay in the country, this made me more than a little nervous. Still I continued to see him because it was novel, because the sex was fun, and because I knew my parents would be horrified. With Marcus I had hit the taboo triumvirate: he was foreign, he was married, and he was black.

Marcus was obsessed with, not me, but the person in his dream. When I gave him the only flattering photo of me extant, he looked at it with disappointment and said, "That's not the face in the dream."

"Well, it's me." I said.

Our relationship was carried on in snatches of the daylight hours during the work week. When I refused to sit all day by my computer on weekends, waiting for his wife to use the bathroom so he could e-mail me a brief line, Marcus complained that I wasn't available enough to him.

"Me not available?" I asked, incredulously. "You are married, for god's sake."

He told me that some configuration in my astrological chart suggested that perhaps I was too stubborn to be in a relationship with a man. This was something my mother had often told me except she got it from God, not an astrology chart.

But I laughed, "Well, I suppose it depends on whether the man is strong enough to handle it. And by the way, you are no one to be calling another person stubborn." Neither, of course, was my mother.

Marcus talked endlessly about me having his child but I did not want a baby at all, let alone with a man who was married to someone else and who didn't seem interested in actually raising a child. When I told him quite bluntly to shut up about me becoming pregnant, he began getting sloppy about condoms. That was the end of the sex for me. It wasn't fun anymore.

But it was amusing to think of the phone call to my parents if Marcus were to see his dream realized: "I'm calling from Ghana…I've married a black man but it's only legal in Africa because he is still married to someone in the U.S. . . . . You have a grandchild." It was almost worth throwing my entire life away.

We were a doomed experiment in international relations from the start, but I didn't know that until an afternoon we spent at Seattle Center. I was driving—since Marcus didn't know how—and looking for a four hour parking space. I kept passing 2-hour signs.

Finally Marcus said, "How will anyone know?"

"Because they chalk the tires." Then I had to explain what that meant.

And in that moment, I saw that this was what life would be like for me if we actually managed to stay together, even with the controlling, the manipulations and the fights about pregnancy. Marcus wasn't stupid, far from it. But there was a world of things he didn't know about western culture and any woman involved with him would necessarily be his teacher. No matter how I reasoned with myself, it still felt like taking care of an adult who was old enough to take care of himself. I was done with that. I broke up with him.

Naked

ENTER MARGY. She was flamboyant, big hearted, and In Charge. She took me under her wing and into her circle. I satellited around her. In my *mappa mundi*, this was the only other alternative to caretaking: hitch myself up to someone who seemed to function better than I did and hope some of it rubbed off. Neither mode worked well for me but I had a lot of fun with Margy.

For several years I joined a group of Margy's friends who spent fall and spring equinoxes at La Push on the Washington coast. La Push is a Native American fishing village that had, at the time, a rustic and rudimentary arrangement of affordable beach cottages. We loaded up the car with food and bedding, took the ferry across Puget Sound, and drove over the top of the Olympia Peninsula to the ocean.

When we got to La Push, we immediately headed to the docks to see what was coming off the fishing boats. We bought live Dungeness crab that were so large we walked them back on leashes. Dropping them into the pot always gave me a shudder, but I learned how to clean them out after they were cooked. The meat was white and sweet, there's nothing like it anywhere else on earth.

There were three of us the first time we went to LaPush: Margy, myself, and a woman named Lisa. We went to the beach in the afternoon of a brilliantly sunny autumn day that belied the coldness of the water. Margy took one look at the sparkling surf and declared,

"I'm fucking going in naked!"

I made one brief reconnaissance glance around; there didn't seem to be anyone else on the beach. "I'll go with you!" I said

We stared hard at each other, and then made a dash to the water's edge where we pulled off our clothes. Hand in hand, we splashed in. It was fucking freezing! We sat down in two feet of water, jumped up, and ran back to where Lisa stood with the towels. There was the sound of clapping. I looked up to see 75 people on a beach that a minute earlier appeared to have been secluded. The experience—including the applause—left me completely exhilarated.

At the vernal Equinox the following year, we did an initial naked run into the water in the afternoon and got bolder in the evening. We made a bonfire on the beach and grilled sea bass we'd gotten at the docks. The sun set, I played my guitar and sang a few songs. Margy and Lisa began drumming. I took off my T-shirt and bra and began to dance.

"C'mon, Margy," I said

"I don't know," she said. "It's a little cold."

"You know, I didn't hear you whining about the cold when we were here before. As I recall you couldn't wait to get naked."

She pulled off her top.

"You know what?" I said. "I'd like to go the full Monty."

No one spoke. Lisa stood up and began fumbling with her belt buckle. Encouraged, I pulled everything off. The next thing, we were all completely naked, dancing with the drums and the rattle, reaching out to the ocean and the stars, feeling like we might vibrate right into the moon. We danced until it hurt to continue flopping around. I didn't feel the same extravagant freedom when I had to hold onto my breasts.

After that, we spent every Equinox weekend more naked than not. I ceremoniously took off all my clothes as soon as the car came off the ferry while we were still two hours from La Push. We threw on clothes to get down to the beach, find a semi-protected spot, and off everything would come. People who came strolling by closer than we thought necessary were pronouced Pervs.

"It's the pheromones," Margy intoned. "It draws them."

She was earthy and irreverent and I liked that. Once I had a yeast infection and had temporarily to use sanitary napkins instead of tampons.

They were itchy and uncomfortable and I imagined I could smell blood. My mother would have asked me to smell her.

I said to Margy, "I feel like people can smell me."

"I can't smell anything," she said. "But that blood running down your leg is kind of off-putting."

Between Margy and Marcus, my sexual pendulum got to swinging. I swung from feeling like a sexual block of wood to being someone who could rip off her clothes at the beach and have sex with a married man. I even posed naked several times for Margy's male artist friend to sketch.

Margy and I weren't so copacetic about spiritual matters. She was involved in Native American spirituality and she romanticized La Push because it was on an Indian reservation. Margy did pipe ceremonies, which everyone in her circle except me participated in. She used a pipe she had been Gifted With and never missed an opportunity to say so. I wanted to scream, "Why can't you just say it was a gift?" It sounded too much like Fellowshipping in evangelical circles.

I was put off by the religious talk. The tone of voice Margy assumed when she talked about the pipe sounded too much like my mother's pious praying. Lisa explained to me—several times and in all earnestness— that if she just kept doing the pipe and going to the sweat lodge over and over, she would finally be purified spiritually. She also told me that she wasn't allowed at native sweats if she were menstruating.

"It grounds the power," she said.

I rolled my eyes. Not because it was any stranger than any other religious belief but because she talked as if there was no other explanation for why women were marginalized in some of the Native American practices. She'd start over, "You see, Elena it's Because. It. Grounds. The. Power."

All religious enthusiasts sound the same: humorless reverence underscores the conviction that enlightenment or Nirvana or salvation or purification is possible if they just believe what they are told. So here I was again, trying to snag a family and a mother and finding a religious system coming between us.

Margy didn't mind my not wanting to be part of her pipe group; she was generous about that. Our point of tension lay elsewhere. She was fierce about her abilities as a mother. She got a rush from being the cool mom, the kind of mom who might leave dinner guests at her table to drive to Northgate Mall, pick up her kids at the Nordstrom end and drive them around to the J. C. Penney end, all because they didn't want to walk. She seemed to be at her children's disposal 24-hours a day. This priority made it hard to carry on an adult friendship.

In any case, I would rather her children stayed at the mall when I was with Margy because I found it increasingly difficult to be around them. There's no doubt there was competition going on between them and me for Mom's attention. Finally I told Margy that I found her household "too stimulating," congratulating myself on my tact, even though we both knew exactly what I meant. I saw less and less of my friend.

The day came when I was able to work myself into a self-righteous lather over all the unspoken hurts and imbalances of the relationship. I wrote Margy one of my famous letters: all empathy shoved aside, it criticized her religious beliefs, her mothering and the eventual outcome of her children. As soon as I mailed the letter, my back went into a spasm that put me in bed for three weeks. Margy didn't speak to me for months. When we did talk, the rupture was irreparable and the relationship ended.

She may never forgive me for criticizing her children, but I doubt she'll forget how much fun we had at La Push. Margy and I will always have Naked.

The Soy Fudge Episode

SIX MONTHS AFTER *I* VISITED FRANCES IN TEXAS, I got the call that she had died. Distraught, I reached out to my parents, whom I hadn't seen in nearly three years. They came to Seattle to see me. It felt good to talk to my father about Frances; it was his younger brother she had married. The three of us went out to lunch. In addition to all my back problems, I now had TMJ, my tally of root canals was at nine; and I had a bunch of food sensitivities, allergies, and digestive problems. I was again one of those stock characters that everyone wants to murder. This time I was the person who is always fussing about her diet and her body pains.

When we ordered our lunch, all my food sensitivities got an airing. My mother immediately wanted to know if there was something she could make for me to eat. I was surprised and touched. I said that I would love some non-dairy fudge. She'd need to use soy milk and safflower margarine; put that way, it didn't sound all that good, but the idea that my mother wanted to make something for me—something I actually wanted—made me glow on the inside. My mother wrote down the ingredients. I mailed her a bag of vegan chocolate chips so she wouldn't have to hunt for them in Olympia.

I made a special trip to my parents' home in Olympia to collect on my fudge, my mother-daughter bonding object. My mother was thrilled to be able to give me something that I appreciated. My father was thrilled that my mother and I weren't fighting. We sat down for lunch.

"Here's your sandwich and these are apples for you. Your dad has some oranges over here, but you can have those if you want. There's egg and a slice of beef in it. Don't you like beef? Well, give it to your dad. How do you get your protein? Where's my napkin? Chuck! Bring the salt and pepper. Do you want something to drink? There's pop but it isn't cold, you don't drink juice, do you? Oh, you do? Just water? I can get the juice. Is that enough? There's more bread. What can I get you?"

"Can I get some soy milk for my tea?"

Her face went blank. "I don't have any soy milk."

"There wasn't any left over from the fudge?"

"I don't think I put soy milk in the fudge."

"What kind of milk did you use?"

"I don't know. Canned milk."

I stared at her. I said slowly, "You were supposed to use soy milk so I could eat it."

"Well, try some. See if you can tell the difference."

"*That's not the point!*"

Her face looked stunned for about five seconds. Her expression teetered on the edge of the decision over what to say next. Whatever she didn't say took massive amounts of energy to suppress. It all played across her face.

She finally lashed out, "You have no idea how much I have to do, how busy I am, how much was on my mind this month. You don't know what my life is like."

I was so disappointed I couldn't stop myself: I locked myself in the bathroom and sobbed.

"I didn't do it on purpose, "she yelled through the door. "*And I have always loved you!*"

I splashed water on my face, blew my nose and came back out. My father had disappeared into the den, but my mother was waiting for me.

"Where is it that Mai works?" she asked conversationally.

But I soldiered on, "Look, you wrote down the ingredients. You said you wanted to do this for me."

"Your problem is," she cast about for one of her lines. "You won't let me help you."

I exploded, "What more could I have done? Bought all the ingredients, made the fudge, poured it in the pan, cut it up, wrapped it, presented it to me and then told you how nice it was of you to do this for me?"

Suddenly I felt I had two choices. I could slice her up in little pieces, put her through the Cuisinart and splash her all over the house or I could get out immediately. I walked out, her voice following me to my car,

"I don't know why you have to act like this!"

I didn't sleep or even stop shaking for nearly a week. My friends told me that it sounded like my mother was a little deranged, no matter that I was the one who felt that way. None of that was the point. I only had one mother and I wanted from her the one thing only she could give: enough attention and love, undiluted by any other concerns, that I could grow up loving myself and feeling reasonably safe in the world. Or something like that. It didn't matter how one described it. It was that thing that when you got it, you knew you had gotten your birthright. And if you didn't have your birthright, you had nothing at all. It didn't matter that I was in my 40s and it was far too late. That didn't stop the needing or the wanting.

Green Rose

I PICKED UP A COPY of *Women Who Run with the Wolves* by Clarissa Pinkola Estes in a waiting room and curled up in a chair. The book fell open to the chapter about the motherless ugly duckling, about finding belonging. I read the chapter and something inside me came alive.

The story was alive. It was my story—or one of them—and it was living its life in me. It was completely believable that because the duckling found who she was and the family to whom she belonged, I would, too. I didn't have to work at it because the story was transpiring. I somehow knew—I instantly believed—that all that was required of me was to pay attention to my own life.

Stories. Myths. They are alive. Their hearts beat in us. They breathe in and out of us. They aren't instructional. They don't need morals tacked onto the ends of them. That's what killed the Bible stories of my childhood. The moralizing foreclosed on the meaning and it's the meaning that's alive. Because it's alive, it's different for everyone.

The power of the duckling myth wrenched open a space in my mind that had clamped shut from too much Sunday school and too much mother. It was a space not available to me in France where I had felt intense homesickness and confusion and which had been met by such condemnation in the Christian community. There was a myth for my experience in France: A longing for home, whether a spiritual home, a childhood home or some remembered place of comfort. A myth had been alive inside of me, straining to break from its moral prison and enter a room where it had space to breathe and where meaning could be found, not imposed.

Between the questions, puzzles, and suffering of life and any reconciliation, acceptance or relief was a space waiting for visitations of desire, love, sadness, mystery and surprise. The space was reminiscent of the picaresque qualities of a Bach invention. The Baroque space, swirling with surprises, between the statement of the theme and the recapitulation, had intrigued me all my life. Myths were in the space. They were stories that were happening right now, every day, to me and to everyone I knew. The stories provided a structure that might possibly keep me from spilling out onto the floor once and for all.

I sold my townhouse in Bothell, bought a quirky house in the Crown Hill neighborhood of Seattle and went back to see Doug. He wasn't a Jungian, but he trafficked in the same neighborhood as the myths: the unconscious.

It had been several years but I still knew his number by heart.

He still answered the phone the same way, "This is Doug."

"Umm, hi. It's me. Elena."

Warmth came through the receiver, "Well, hi!"

But something was different. He was now driving the first in a series of black Volvo station wagons. There was a couch in his office. He seemed different, rather like his new vehicle and the black couch: solid, secure, safe. As if before his bones had been hollow, and now they were dense with blood and marrow. As if before he had been taking short, shallow sips of air, and now the air was flowing leisurely in and out. A candidate to become a psychoanalyst, he was in the middle of his own analysis. As we settled into a routine, his transformation continued right before my eyes. He was more comfortable in his own skin. He was mellower, gentler, more apt to laugh, and to smile.

"I am only coming once a week," I declared.

"That's ok,"

"I don't want to get attached."

We looked at each other. We both knew the attachment was still there: complex, intense, and compelling.

The old subject of The Incident came up, the time I drove by his house. In a comical reversal of sensibilities, he told me he wouldn't mind if I knew where he lived now.

"Hell, I'll give you my address," he said.

"You know what? No thank you. I prefer to not know!" I said.

I didn't want his address. I wanted my own. I was still the ugly duckling looking for a place to belong. My birth was Caesarian so leaving the womb wasn't natural. ("You can't let go of the kids," my father yelled. "They had to *cut* them out of you.") My parents clutched at me every time I tried to leave home. The church, my replacement home, had not accepted me so I had wrenched myself away from Christianity.

Psychoanalysis became my spiritual home. Analysis is quite different from psychotherapy not the least because you spend so much time in the consulting room, you want to leave your toiletries. The topic of analysis floated obliquely into the conversation one day.

I stared silently at the couch for a good long stretch.

"I wouldn't want you sitting behind me. I would want to turn my head to look at you once in a while." I said.

"Yeah, that would be better for you."

I decided to start analysis. It was a decision to not only become more attached to Doug, but to crawl all the way inside the dependence and out the other side. After his own analysis, Doug was less constrained by his own leashes. He welcomed more counter-transference into our conversations, rather than trying to pretend it didn't have influence. Because this rang true with my perceptions, I was willing to trust him more, inch by inch.

I had four sessions a week for five years. I lay on the couch that first session and asked, "How is this going to be different than therapy?"

"I don't know."

Doug absolutely believed in the process, even though he had no idea where it was going. Philosophically, I believed in the process, but it scared the hell out of me. Years before, in therapy, I had specific problems I wanted solved. Sometimes I wrote them down. Sometimes I wrote pages and pages of stuff and read them aloud to Doug.

"This is what I feel, what I just read. What do you think?"

"About what?" he asked, maddeningly.

In analysis, I realized that it was more valuable to not plan anything. Just go in and say the first thing that came to mind. It was interesting how frightening this was. Then I got to a point where there was a detached curiosity about my own feelings and thoughts. Beyond that was an eagerness to discover what my unconscious would serve up next.

I learned to surrender to whatever happened in a moment whether it was silence or me saying something or Doug bringing his otherness into my awareness. I learned that our two minds could meander along wherever they took us and that after enough rambling, I would end up someplace where I wanted to be. I couldn't control where that would be and neither could Doug. I discovered capacities I didn't know I had for gratitude and forgiveness, sexual fantasies that no longer frightened me, anger that felt manageable, and a kaleidoscope of motives that accompanied everything I did. As analysis progressed, I became calmer and felt more substantial.

I lost fifty pounds without going on a diet, almost without noticing it. In a Bon Marche dressing room, pulling on a skirt two sizes smaller than the last time I bought a skirt, I marveled, "When did this happen?" It happened mysteriously, as a side effect of exploring the meaning I made of my experiences and memories of food and of eating.

Some things, however, were still intractable. I was still trying to make Doug be the parent who would give me what I needed to have my own life. I persisted in thinking it was possible to get it from someone other than myself.

"Your stubbornness is not helping you," he said, exasperated.

"You used to call me tenacious. You thought it was a good thing."

"Yeah, now I am calling it stubbornness."

"Well, we're well matched."

I persisted in trying to impress him with my abilities and talent, still imagining that I would feel loved when he acknowledged how extraordinary I was.

One day I read him a poem I had written.

"That doesn't do anything for me," he said.

I could feel the shame when it was still a distance away. I could feel it leering at me through the French glass doors that opened into a little courtyard. It swelled the door open and gushed towards me, carrying pieces of jagged glass and laughing maniacally.

"That's not the point," I gasped. "It's not about what it "does" for you."

We stared at each other. There was a lot of shame in the room. I didn't know it then, but Doug was having his own bout of it. He was repeating a scene from his own analysis, one that had gone undigested until it he regurgitated it in my session.

"I've had it," I said. "I'm not coming back."

You go off psychoanalysis like you do a drug. You have to ramp it down so you don't go into withdrawal. But the next few sessions were awful.

Finally, Doug said, "Okay, I think we should just stop." He spread his hands. "I've failed you. I have approached you every way I could think of, done everything I know how to do, and nothing has worked. I don't want you to leave, but I don't have anything left." He looked defeated. He looked vulnerable.

In that moment, I felt loved and for once, I let it sink in. His vulnerability made everything look different to me. We had been two prisms sitting across from each other, always reflecting the same facets. In that moment of humility he had turned slightly in his chair so the reflections were different and all the ways he had loved me suddenly shone; all the times I had hurt him and he had not retaliated. Every time a clog got unstuck in me, it could be traced back to some risk Doug had taken in the relationship, some vulnerability I had been too frightened to be conscious of.

We stayed with it and the next year—my final year—was like inhabiting a poem. A poet pays attention to small things. I discovered that when I paid attention to every moment, I went into a flow. I had big, noisy feelings. What happened in analysis was subtle and small: shafts of the light playing across facets of memory and feelings, calling to other facets deep in the prisms of two human beings, illuminating without defining. When Doug and I talked, we noticed small things for no other reason than to notice.

With no apologies to Sigmund Freud, what happened to me in analysis was, at its core, spiritual. Sometimes it seemed like there was just one mind and it wasn't in either of us, it was in the room somewhere. The space that the myths had found in my mind was also a space between me and another person. Our minds meandered together in space and time, creating a place of surprise where I learned what I didn't know I knew; and what I thought I knew, I didn't know; and where I wondered what it meant to know anything at all. Where what I said was what the other was thinking but the other was thinking it because of something I said.

Where the other is both someone in the room but also someone in my mind.

I came to think of this meandering mind as an ocean of images, associations, patterns, ideas, memories, dreams; as something ineffable, something greater than myself, greater than all of us, unknowable, unending. It was within me all the time yet I couldn't contain it. It held all my love, shame, fear, sadness and delight. It let those feelings seep into my awareness only as much as I could cope with them. It could blast into my conscious mind via a dream. Or speak in a still, small voice, telling me of my desire. It could be influenced by other minds. I called it my Unknown Familiar.

Up until my analysis, I had thought, "No matter what good things happen to me in my life, I still would rather be dead, if only I could just follow through with it." After analysis, I thought, "No matter what difficult things happen to me, I want to be alive. I want my life."

I made the decision to leave analysis. Doug's office had been a womb for me, a place where the air I breathed had already cycled once through him. Now the cloister felt claustrophobic. I felt like an 18-year-old who was itching to leave home. I knew I could always go back for a visit. I could even go back and do therapy or another analysis if I ever had enough money, ever again. But it was important to me to have an experience of leaving. It felt good. I felt like a grownup.

Nowadays, I hang out in the intersection of psychoanalysis, Buddhism and Christianity, trying not to get hit. I include Christianity in the intersection because I recognize that I can't expunge it from my personality. It is part of my memory and the stuff of my soul. The archetypes are all there, as well as the words to some really gruesome hymns. I believe this is unavoidable. We can't expunge. We have to integrate. My lapsed Catholic friends may change their names to Sunshine or Abdul, but they still manage to find a Pope wherever they go. If they are lucky, the Virgin Mary makes herself irresistible to them, and they allow her to knit together some of the ragged pieces of their past.

I came to admit that I never had anything against Jesus Christ. From a psychoanalytic point of view, I might say that Mary and Joseph did a pretty decent job for him to have the self-image he had. They were good enough parents. I came to believe that Jesus showed a new way to make sense of what it meant to be born and to be a person; a way to grow into the glory of one's own life. The point was not to copy his life. He was a mystic with some remarkable insights about what it meant to be alive, and a stunning ability with language and metaphor. I found a way to fit him into my own private pantheon.

My friend Joan said: "For Jesus to continue the road he was on, he was going to run into trouble. He could have avoided it. He could have gone to Greece. But to be the person he believed himself to be, he had to do what he did."

It's no different for any of us. We all either stay on our road, or we escape ourselves and go to Greece.

I am no longer fluent in the Christian language, but when I hear Christians talk about how much they love the Lord, I understand them to be talking about their experience of the Divine. I imagine that they had an explosive experience around the person of Jesus Christ much in the same way I had an explosive experience around the concepts of myths and the unconscious. I believe we are excited about the same phenomena but are expressing it in different languages.

I left analysis with one absolute: I can believe anything I want to believe. No person alive knows what happens after death but I am the only person alive who knows what it feels like to be me on earth right now. After analysis, I was curious rather than frightened about what Life would present to me.

In the Midst of Life

ANNA AND JULIA ELLERMEIER WERE IN ELEMENTARY SCHOOL when they started piano lessons with me. Imaginative, funny, and full of love, they were touchers, something I wasn't used to, and I always felt a little glow of surprise after one of their spontaneous hugs. In the beginning, Anna, the older sister, was shy and self-conscious, and Julia was the big personality. Julia tended to answer all questions, whether directed to her or not. Lessons were full of cross-talk, sister infighting, and laughter.

When their father, Dennis, brought them to their lessons, he popped in to say hello and chat with me. The week before Christmas, I ditched the piano lessons and the four of us sang Christmas carols together. Dennis had a magnificent tenor voice. I liked his cheerfulness—so different from my own tendencies—and I noticed that he asked me about me; he didn't just yak about himself.

One October, when Anna was 15 and Julia was 11, Dennis was diagnosed with terminal melanoma and suddenly he was dying. Now when I sat with his girls at their lessons, I watched their faces and tears welled up in my eyes. I began going to their house instead of them coming to me because that was one less thing for their mother, Yetta, to cope with. No one wanted to discontinue the lessons, but we were all less exuberant.

Dennis was home from the hospital for Christmas. A group of neighbors and friends got together a caroling party. They asked me to make song sheets and lead the singing. We got ourselves organized at the traffic circle a few doors down from the Ellermeiers. The whole block was alight with Christmas lights on a dry, clear evening. Dennis sat on the porch in a wheelchair, smiling and waving; full of enthusiasm, full of life.

Afterwards, I talked with him. He was propped up in a wheelchair and hooked up to various apparatus. He had lost the use of most of his body so when he waved to us, one hand worked the other arm. He was on heavy pain medication. But there was still laughter in his eyes. I asked him what he was savoring about being home and he loved the question. He said he was savoring watching his girls. Anna was adolescing and her humor was sharp and funny; her self-confidence flowering. Dennis said he was sorry he wouldn't be there to see Julia grow into a frank, sarcastic adolescent, which, I might add, she did. I told Dennis that I would stay in his daughters' lives as long as they wanted me.

The atmosphere around Dennis, as he slumped in the wheelchair, was rich, like a reduced sauce. It was pure, condensed Life. As we talked and he, characteristically, asked about me, I felt as though a transaction took place. It was as if Dennis said to me, "Look, I have all this Life that I am not going to be needing anymore, because I am dying, so please, take it. Take as much as you want."

I took. Just as I had done with Meagan, my fourteen-year-old student with the brain tumor, I let in as much as I could. I didn't know what it meant. I wasn't even sure what I was doing. I sensed that all I needed was to be open to whatever was happening. It was an omen, like the rainbow on the beach at Looe. It was a coda to the symphony of analysis. Life was available to me, who had so often wanted to die.

Dennis died the following month. I think of our transaction sometimes when I get frightened, when I get existential angst, and it still comforts and reassures me.

My own father died almost exactly a year later on another cold January day. Early one morning in his 93rd year, he had a stroke and fell on the bathroom floor. Driving to Olympia that day, I felt nostalgic for the father who had given me my sense of humor. I missed Arthur and the ridiculous banter we could engage in for hours while my mother read her Bible and tried to pretend she didn't feel left out. I felt nostalgic for that time in my teens when I had him all to myself, cordoned off by recognition of the price I had paid, before my various disassociated parts cut the rope line and began informing on each other.

The hospital room seemed the saddest place on earth. My mother was in shock. My brother, whom I hadn't seen in years, had little to say to anyone.

My father gasped for air in an oxygen mask; all life support had been removed. I sat on the bed and sang a song that he and I had laughed about over the years: "When the Foemen Bares His Steel" from the Gilbert and Sullivan operetta *The Pirates of Penzance.*

On the D'Oyly Carte recording, the major general sends the troops off to war by singing: "Go ye heroes, go and die!" The heroes march in place, singing, "We go, we go." The major general, whines in exasperation, "Yes, but you *don't* go! Damme, you *DON'T* go!"

When I got to that part in the song, I realized that I was singing more than a favorite song. My father was trying to die, wanting to die, and I was singing, "Yes, but you *don't* die!" He managed a small smile and put his hand on mine. It meant a great deal to me that the last thing I shared with my father was a favorite joke.

After our father died, Alex and I tried e-mailing to get better acquainted. When I am in a charitable frame of mind, I describe my brother like this: He is an artist. He plays the piano, beautifully and enviably, by ear. He is a potter. His pots are amazing in their imaginative delicacy. He thinks like an artist. He has that messy kind of mind that is a pile of ashes from which a phoenix arises. He approaches life in a gullible, guileless way. His sensibilities are like wind chimes, apt to shatter in the face of conflict. I feel like a Machiavellian clod of earth next to him.

From the e-mail correspondence, I finally understood the source of his dislike of me. Because I had hung around home rather than cut myself off from our parents, he assumed I had gotten, at his expense, all the goodies our parents had to give. I sat in an Easter basket of sweet love, understanding, and approval. In other words, I had the birthright. Like I was frigging Jacob and I had gotten The Blessing. I think he understood intellectually that we both had been screwed, but grief is not something you can think yourself out of. With our father gone, he was running out of receptacles for his own rage and sadness.

I was flabbergasted. I tried to explain what I had been through trying to put together my life, but he couldn't hear it. His anxiety made his writing incoherent. He needed a therapist, not a sister. The e-mailing petered out. It was too painful and we were too far in arrears.

I was now without a father and for all intents and purposes, I was out one brother. I was down to a mother I didn't want to be around but who was still part of me whether I liked it or not, and I didn't. My mother had showed a nascent talent for painting in her old age so as a way of trying to integrate what could not be expunged, I learned to paint.

The first time I tried watercolor, I was enchanted with the way the paint ran down the wet paper and made patterns, puddles and rivulets. I was fascinated with the way one color discharged other colors, creating new ones that bloomed and bled. It was fun to get out of the way and watch. I bought a children's book and worked straight through it.

I learned as much as I could on my own, then I went looking for help. I asked questions of artists. I took a year of drawing classes. I took a few private painting lessons. Finally, I found a teacher, Molly Hashimoto, and studied with her for two years. She was a wonderful first teacher. She made suggestions, but mostly she left me alone to do the kinds of experimental things I wanted to do and helped me when I asked for help. I liked wet in wet, loose painting and I painted fast. I liked to do the same scene ten times, just to see how many different ways it might come out.

One day, as I started in on my fourth painting in an hour's time, Molly said to me, "I can tell you are a musician. You do your paintings in time." I glowed with pleasure. She had seen and acknowledged me with an insight that hadn't occurred to me and that I had forgotten was part of me.

I was a musician. Where had that gone? I loved teaching but that wasn't the same as being inside my own music. The desire to sing was still an old ache and a tired companion. My voice is like that pilot light that won't go out.

The Stars of the Morning

THOMASA ECKERT—TOMMIE—WAS LIKE NO TEACHER I had ever had. She was the first music teacher in forty years whom I was not afraid of. She was the first voice teacher whose singing voice I loved. My other teachers had good, trained voices, capable of doing technical things that I wanted to learn to do. But I never fell in love with their sound. Even in demonstrations or in those bursts that singers are prone to, as though to check that The Voice is still there, Tommie's voice sang to my heart.

At my first lesson I met a nationally known soprano and pianist. She was wearing a blue sweatshirt over which she had thrown a yellow smocked sundress, black leggings and white Nike running shoes. Tommie had grown up amongst the turbans and caftans of New York City's 1950's classical vocal scene. This was her version of their eccentric dress.

She greeted me like she had been waiting her whole life for me to walk into her studio, and as though she had nothing to do on that day except to spend an hour with me. A calmness seemed to follow her around and leave little pockets of itself everywhere.

Tommie wanted to hear me sing. I had brought "The Jauchzet," the Bach cantata for soprano that I had sung twelve years earlier. I had no idea if I could still sing it but it was on top of the stack of music I had brought with me. She sat at the piano, her glasses perched on her nose so she could look through them to read her music and look over them to see me. A sight-reading wizard, her tiny hands moved across the keys like a flock of hummingbirds. She blitzed through the introduction and away we went. I was surprised at how easily the first aria came back. When we finished, she said, "As soon as you started to sing, I thought, 'Oh. She has a gift.'" I got tears in my eyes.

I knew hundreds of classical songs and had been an accomplished singer at one time. But I didn't want to work on repertoire. I wanted to know why I got vocally tired and why my singing had been as much a source of anxiety as joy. In many ways I had never gotten over the trauma of having a vocal nodule when I was sixteen.

I didn't sing another song for a year. I spent three months lying on the floor, making interesting sounds; then nine months singing everything on "ooh." I hung upside down and sang. I put on funny hats and masks and sang. I danced around the room, waved my arms, stood on one foot, and sang.

Sometimes I sang a phrase and reported that I didn't like the way it sounded.

"Make it sound worse," Tommie said. "Go into the middle of those awful sounds."

Every sound had its own peculiar beauty. I whined; I wailed. I broke down and cried in the middle of a wail because it unlodged something deep within me.

"Support every sound with the breath," she said. "Let's just see what's there."

I sang a pitch, went slightly sharp, then slightly flat; just a quarter tone, not even a half step. The sound glowed like a star.

"Sometimes you have to go to the far edges to find the center," Tommie said.

This wasn't just about singing. This was something profound about life. The words reverberated in my mind in tandem with the vibrations in my body.

I learned to stay with a single pitch, listening and feeling its evolution. A single tone has colors, layers and depths. I felt tiny spinning vibrations in my head that connected me with something ancient as though the sound swept into my head on winds from long ago.

Like inhabiting a poem in psychoanalysis, I could inhabit a tone with my voice. A single tone could be an intricate cave to explore. An ooh vowel could be a vessel on which I might take an entire journey. I learned to roll sounds around the cavities of my head, going where my voice wanted to go, rather than directing it somewhere. I let tones find their way wherever it felt easy and free; wherever I got a buzz or where it reverberated like a Tibetan singing bowl. It was both exhilarating and relaxing. A voice lesson with Tommie was an hour of massage, meditation, and time travel.

All the unusual things I tried in voice lessons were not just techniques. They grew out of Tommie's own struggles in life, her own reflectiveness, her Buddhist orientation, her belief in love, her confidence in the process of listening and paying attention to what's there, and her understanding that every sound, like every moment, was worth noticing.

In psychoanalytic sessions my mind meandered through the previously unthinkable the way my voice did in working with Tommie. I explored a tone, rolling it around in my mouth, deep in my throat, up behind my eyes, in my nose, and on my teeth. It was like watching uncontrolled paint run down wet Arches paper. In the formerly unthinkable, on the far edges of the worst sounds and in the uncontrollable run of the paint, there, *there* were the stars of the morning, shining in their beauty, illuminating the many possibilities of what it meant to be alive.

In both singing and analysis I got acquainted and somewhat comfortable with the feeling of not knowing. Not knowing what sound was going to come out, not knowing what an eventual outcome would be, not knowing what one small thing had to do with anything else. I felt more confident that whatever sound came out, I could continue to send air into it and it would sing itself. I felt more confident that the small moments of life would sing themselves into a song if I only just paid attention and loved each note.

Kathie

I WALKED MY MOTHER DOWN HER STREET to an all-neighborhood yard sale where we met its instigator, Kathie, an energetic, cheerful woman a few years older than me, with a huge smile and red hair. Kathie took a shine to my mother, called her "Miss Mary," and soon began popping in once a day to check on her.

She was leaving my mother's house as I was coming in one fall afternoon. The house smelled like someone had died several days earlier and was decomposing in the back bedroom. I sniffed my way into the kitchen where I saw swarms of flies hovering over various piles of open garbage and rotting food. This was worse than when I was growing up. I swept everything into the garbage and emptied the whole mess into the can outside. I rinsed out the pail and sprayed it with one of the 14 partially used bottles of toxic cleaning solutions under the kitchen sink.

"Why didn't you ask Kathie to empty the garbage for you?"

"Oh, no," my mother frowned. "She was my guest."

I understood instantly that Kathie had offered to help and my mother had refused her help. As unreasonable as it was, Kathie had respected that. But she had the same itch to get into the house as I had. A month later when my mother went into hospice with metastasized pancreatic cancer, Kathie offered to clean out the house and run the estate sale.

"Are you kidding?" I asked. "Absolutely! We should sit down and talk about how much you want to be paid."

"I don't want anything," she said. "I love your mother. I want to do this for her. And I've done a lot of estate sales. I can give you references."

Kathie was the mysterious stranger who appears on the sidelines of a tragedy and works magic. When my mother was dying, Kathie was everywhere, quietly doing what needed to be done, without calling attention to herself. One afternoon at the hospice I met her coming out of my mother's room. In one hand was an aluminum foil parcel, in the other a razor. She handed me a batch of molasses ginger cookies; chewy, with sugar on top, extra ginger flavor.

She waved the razor: "I wanted to get this done before you got here," she said. "Miss Mary's been fussing about a little mustache."

I flashed back to when I had to squeeze my mother's blackheads and scratch her dandruff and I shuddered. A halo gleamed above Kathie's head and stigmata appeared on her hands and feet.

My brother came for our mother's burial. He and I had a brief moment of agreement when we discussed what to do with her King James Bible. I had uncovered about 25 Bibles in the house. Some of them, like the little white one she carried at her wedding, and her childhood Bible with Mary Kiosse stamped on the front cover, were rather sweet. But the Bible we had seen her read while we were growing up, the one she had bludgeoned us with, the one that was still her favorite, her King James Version, made me shudder. I would have liked to rip it apart page by page until I had a funeral pyre like I had done with my New American Standard, but I couldn't bring myself to destroy this one. Neither of us wanted it, and selling it or giving it away was unthinkable, so we buried it with her, commenting ruefully that it was the only thing she had ever seemed to love.

My mother looked very sweet in death. With all her fight drained out of her, her expression matched a photo of her when she was twelve years old, shyly fingering flowers in her mother's garden.

I got a visitation from my mother a few months after her death. I had taken a copy of her death certificate to my bank along with a check for $300 made out to Mary K. Richmond. The check was from a class action law suit against one of many semi-criminal organizations that manipulate money out of elderly people in the form of "pledges." Her mail was coming to my house while I tried to get her name off close to 500 of these organizations. I knew on sight which mail to throw in the recycle en route from the mail box to my front door, and which inspired further investigation. I had opened this particular letter. I got together the documents and walked to the bank where they seemed unconcerned about cashing the check.

On my way home, I came through the cemetery. It was a cold winter day and there was an unusual amount of snow lying around Seattle. As I rounded a corner, I saw a shadow come up behind me so I moved to let whoever it was pass. No one passed. When I turned around there was no one in sight, but there was a momentary glint of sun on a piece of ice, high in a bare tree. It blinded me for a second, and then was gone. The bare branch waved. I smiled a small smile that slowly got broader until I laughed outright. My first thought was that she was pleased to do this small thing for me from beyond the grave. Then it occurred to me that *of course*, my mother would come checking on what was happening with her money. And finally I heard her voice saying, "There. Don't say I never do anything for you."

By this time, Kathie and I were enthusiastically rooting through the house, wearing respirator masks and latex gloves. Kathie worked like a fiend every evening after work, and I went to Olympia every other weekend. The garage filled with boxes of junk. The rooms of the house filled with boxes labeled "Save." The big dining room table filled with anything that might be considered valuable or collectible: an Ansonia clock, 1920's painted postcards, some quite nice silver. The bedroom wall filled with pictures of Jesus and 27 girdles.

I was grateful beyond anything I could express for her commitment to this massive undertaking. We had some auxiliary help, but otherwise it was Kathie and me in that house. Mostly Kathie. It took us nine months.

When More Than Was Lost Is Found

KATHIE AND I SETTLED ON THE WEEKEND after Memorial Day for "Miss Mary's Shock and Awe Estate Sale of 2008." The advance publicity read:

> Sixty years, three floors, and five bedrooms of glorious junk, collectibles, antiques.
> And 35 boxes of Kleenex!
> One Girdle or One Religious Book Free with Every Purchase! While Supplies Last!

I made name tags for the army of worker bees I brought from Olympia. They all sported a little garter and said things like:

> KATHIE, I'm the Boss.
> ELENA, I'm the Daughter.
> GWEN, I'm the Daughter's Long Suffering Neighbor
> FAWN, Promoted to this from Elected Gov't Official
> NINA, I've known The Daughter for 30 years. I know why she's the Way She Is.
> SANDI, I came for the girdles.

TERRY, I wanted to Torch the Place
JOAN, I Cleaned out the Refrigerator

I made a collection of tags to hand out with purchases: They all said *Miss Mary's Shock and Awe Estate Sale of 2008* with additional tag lines like "I made the First Purchase!" "She was my first grade teacher." "I spent over $100." "I survived it." I made 38, as many tags as I could find garters.

Gwen, my long suffering neighbor with the SUV, drove me to Olympia the day before the Shock and Awe sale. She helped with the final organization and spent the night on the floor of my father's den. "There's a nice energy in here," she told me. That made me smile. It felt like my father had showed up for the last great recycle, the final trip to take out the garbage.

An Estate Sale is a theater where human pettiness is on glorious display, like the comic bits in Shakespeare. We foreclosed on a few of the stock characters with some signs: *Only a body can hold a place in line; if you leave coats and bags, they will be moved aside. If you ring the doorbell before 8 AM, an entire box of religious books will be thrust upon you.*

The characters were lined up outside the house at 6:30 that morning. They waited until we opened the door at 8:00. They swarmed the house. The sale had begun and the characters played their parts.

One woman Nina intercepted not once, but twice, walking off with a crock pot.

"There's a crack in the lid."

"So you think it's free, then?"

There was the woman who bustled over to show me there was a tear in the dress so maybe I would give it to her for half the price.

"I know there's a tear. That's why it's fifty cents."

Someone else didn't want to pay a dollar for a hardback book. "You know, people at other estate sales are willing to bargain."

"OK, how about $2.50? It just went up for you."

There was an annoying woman who circulated the sale, trying to strike separate bargains with everyone wearing a name tag and then coalesce all her various arrangements at checkout, the result being to pay next to nothing at all. She wanted my parent's two hospital beds. She wanted them for exactly half what we were asking. I said No. Kathie said No. Fawn who could stare down a tornado, said No.

Sandi who spent the day at the cash box, her bright pink lipstick growing brighter every time she repeated it, said, "I'm not authorized to bargain."

Annoying Woman pulled me aside and blew her stale coffee breath in my face, "What time are you lowering your prices?"

"We're not," I said. I stepped upwind.

She gave me her card. "If they don't sell," she whispered. "Call me and we'll Work Something Out."

I told Kathie, "I will *give* them away before I'll sell them to her at any price!" In the end, I believe we did give them away. Human pettiness? Full display.

For my money, the star of the show was a friend of my mother's, 90-year-old Barbara, who came to help at about 10:00 in the morning and was still going strong at 5:00, long after the rest of us were lying like a bunch of wet socks all over the few pieces of furniture that hadn't sold. She crept slowly around the house, straightening and rearranging. Indefatigable, she moved an entire bookcase of large books two at a time from one floor to another.

"They weren't selling well in the basement," she explained.

Another friend of my parents said he would take all the books on the porch and all the Bibles. The news traveled through the sale like gossip in a small town: "Someone got all the religious books!"

The girdles went immediately. Everyone wanted one.

The sale was a huge success. Word got around that a *real* Estate Sale was going on; the sale of an actual estate, not what's called an Estate Sale because part of grandma's china is mixed in amongst the coffee mugs and crime fiction. There were never less than fifty people in the house all day long. Quite a few old acquaintances popped in and lots of people who knew my mother and were interested to meet me. I had so much fun, I could have gotten up and done it again the next day.

At the end of the sale, I did one bit of tidying up before I locked the doors on the mess that I would tend to later: I took down the pictures I had taped to the front door: drawings from my mother's first graders. Drawings of Mrs. Richmond with mounds of curly black hair, little eyeglasses and stick legs and arms. A real person had lived here.

An Estate. The tangible residue of a life. The intangible is more than a residue. It's as big and unknowable as the unconscious. All the trips from Seattle to Olympia during the organization of my childhood home had taken on a metaphysic of their own. I wove something as I shuttled back and forth, carrying strands of memory and bits of my family from my childhood home to my present home, weaving them into the stuff of my life now.

I brought home a clock that had hung in the family living room for as long as I could remember. My mother had embroidered a colorful coil of flowers on its fabric face. I wasn't sure I liked it or wanted it. But when I put it on the wall of my home, it looked like it belonged there.

As difficult as my parents had been, I still felt bereft. I grieved not for something I had lost, but for something I would never have. The pain and confusion from my childhood didn't go away, but something inside me stabilized. I wove a cloth strong enough to hold my memories.

An old hymn from the evangelical church days surfaced:

> "It is well, it is well,
>
> With my soul, with my soul,
>
> It is well, it is well,
>
> With my soul."

I started singing that little refrain a lot. I sang it during the day and when I awoke at three in the morning, unable to sleep.

My parents had been preoccupied with each other; neither of them had seemed to understand what it meant that we were children, not miniature adults. Their input mattered. The unconscious communications did the most damage: the shame of being orphaned and the anxiety around sexual attraction to your daughter; the shame of being the child of immigrants, of being sexually molested because you didn't know how to protect yourself; also the need to be vigilant and afraid because the world is an unsafe place.

Because my parents couldn't talk about it, I couldn't afford to think about it. I crawled into my little hole and let an entire society live and move and have its being around my monolith to the unthinkable. If I were to think the unthinkable, it would go something like this: you aren't safe, you aren't loved, what you desire is not important, men will use you, you have to pay attention to what other people want or they won't like you and you'll be alone.

I couldn't know that I had built this monolith as a way to protect my young self; I thought it was just how the world was. I stayed away from people who might cause me to bump against the monolith and to question why it was there. I folded my arms and said stonily to Doug, "All I want is to get out of here without you helping me." I needed people to fit my map of the world. My *mappa mundi*.

On one of my visits to England, I saw the 13th century *mappa mundi* in Hereford Cathedral. It isn't a map in a modern sense; it's more like a mandala in that it can be entered from any point and the journey from that point is different than from any other. The journey is not just one of geography but of belief and culture, an entire world view.

In the bottom right hand corner of the *mappa mundi* is a boy on horseback, riding away from the world. He has turned and is looking back towards the map, waving farewell. Waving farewell to the world. I grew fond of this little figure, this young boy who was riding to something new and different. A new world.

"Hmmm," I thought. "A mappa can change. *I* can make a different map." That became another mantra.

I gave up the fantasy that I would ever get The Big Get. The birthright. The thing that when I had it, I would know it. My parents didn't have any birthrights to give away. They just gave birth to me. They gave me a chance to live. Granted, they also gave me a convoluted map to a psychic labyrinth, left me to find my way through and tried to eat me every step of the way. But there was no way that it was Supposed to Be. There was only the way it was.

Still, that pilot light inside me, my spirit, is inviolate. That's the consolation prize. I get Me. I get the experience of my own life, a full share of desire, joy, and suffering just like everyone else. I have the same terrible freedom to follow my desire and to make my meaning. This means there have been days when I have thrown it all away for a piece of Safeway chocolate cake.

Doug has been there for most of my adult life. Unlike my parents, he was someone who developed. When I first started therapy with him at $30 an hour, he was a bit of a mess himself. We kludged together something that worked. Something mysterious happens in analysis. Two minds, two Unknown Familiars running together like paint down wet paper, mixing images and associations with love until they create something both astonishing and reassuringly human.

Our influences on each other are mysterious. Two people paying attention to small moments can throw off a lifetime's trajectory. Small moments when a shift in the light illuminates something new. A piece of ice, glimmering high in a tree. A star of the morning. A small stranger's condolence card that helpfully adds, "You met me."

Envoi

I didn't recognize you in Hospice.
Yours was not my mother's face,
not because of the loose, yellow skin;
It was a set of your mouth
and the light in your eyes
That was strange.

You asked how I was
(My mother is dying, How do you think I am?)
I said "I'm just living my life."
You said "That's a good thing to do."
Coming from you,
That was strange.

I found a photo
of 12-year-old Mary
In her mother's garden
during a hot Montana summer.
You have that same set of your mouth,
The same bright eyes.

The same bright eyes I see in you
As you lay quietly dying.
Off you go, my mother,
To your new adventure,
Your young eyes full of mischief and promise.
That's a good thing to do.

Elena Louise Richmond
Nov. 27, 2007

My thanks to:

Mary-Ellis Adams and Nancy Kennedy, the earliest encouragers of my writing.

Joan McKiel, Sally Parks, Madelaine Ramey, Susan Towle, and Gwen Howell, the first appreciative readers of this manuscript.

Chris Foss for her encouragement, her several reads, and her eleventh hour, New York proofread.

Karol Marshall and Tamara Gittelson for hours of conversation about psychoanalysis, life, and art.

Nina Christensen for hours of dissection of the subject of mothers and daughters.

Tommie Eckert for her meticulous proofreading and for not making me change her name, much as I would have enjoyed calling her Celestial Seasonings, Cece for short.

Katie Miller for showing me how to use Word.

Tom Orton, editor par excellence, with added thanks for pointing out the chapters that sounded angry and crazed.

The person called Juliet in this story, for our renewed friendship.

Susan Abbe for learning me what a copyeditor do.

ELENA LOUISE RICHMOND lives in Seattle, Washington where she gets into mischief in her Local Dilettante Studio.

www.elenalouiserichmond.com
www.okchoraleseattle.com